65-50

the CHRISTIAN CENTURIES

FRANCES GUMLEY AND BRIAN REDHEAD

the CHRISTIAN CENTURIES

FRANCES GUMLEY AND BRIAN REDHEAD

BBC BOOKS

Published by BBC Books,
a division of BBC Enterprises Limited,
Woodlands, 80 Wood Lane, London W12 0TT
First published 1989

ISBN 0 563 20774 4

Set in 11/13 pt Garamond by Butler & Tanner Ltd,
Frome and London
Printed and bound in Great Britain by Butler & Tanner Ltd,
Frome and London
Colour separations by Technik Ltd, Berkhamsted
Jacket printed by Belmont Press Ltd, Northampton

CONTENTS

·

·

ERRATUM

List of Illustrations

Please note that page numbers should read two pages earlier, e.g. page 11 = page 9 etc.

ILLUSTRATIONS

·

Colour

THE KEY IS CONSTANTINE

On the road to Rome almost seventeen centuries ago, a forty-year-old soldier with political ambitions, blond hair, a broken nose and a reputation for thoroughness, looked up into the sky and claimed he saw a vision which he could not understand.

> *It was afternoon, the sun had begun his slow descent towards evening. I turned my eyes towards the sun's rays when to my surprise I saw a cross of light over the sun and with it was an inscription, 'By this you shall conquer.' I did not know what it meant.*

The soldier was Constantinus, the son of Constantius the Pale. Constantinus is now better remembered as Constantine the Great, the

Constantine, the soldier emperor who was proud of his looks, fond of his mother, politically ambitious and — most important of all — in search of a strong god

unifier of empire, the unlikely friend of those who had suffered for their belief in the man/god broken on a cross nearly three centuries before.

At the time of his vision Constantine was on the brink of immense power. He had already been proclaimed emperor of the countries to the west of the Alps – but that was not enough. As he approached Rome he was ready to do battle with his rival Maxentius for control of Italy. He needed a strong patron god.

That night, as he was later to tell his biographer, the arch-survivor Eusebius, he fell asleep trying to work out the significance of the cross of light. And while he slept, he dreamt and this time he understood. In his dream Christ, the anointed one, appeared to him with the same sign he had seen in the sky that afternoon. From now on, Constantine was told, the sign of the cross was to be his sign. Constantine accepted the instruction without question.

Down the ages many have questioned the authenticity of that vision and dream, a process as useful as trying to tie knots with water. Dreams are impossible to corroborate and visions, no matter how real, are usually subjective. But what cannot be denied is the impact of Constantine's new-found allegiance. There is no country in the world today which has not been affected by it.

It may seem coy and whimsical to begin this journey towards the Middle Ages with a dream and a vision when there is a wealth of more tangible objective evidence available. But there is method in this feyness. We want to follow the paths of men and women of unimaginable temperamental difference: abbesses, harlots, hermits, emperors, geniuses, murderers, madmen and poets; all of them gripped by a story of a life thrown away on a hill outside Jerusalem. This conviction, beyond common sense, will draw men and women across all logical and territorial boundaries – their stories are a history of more than fact. If we want to understand the past we must look to its people and how their faith, visions and dreams have changed and moulded the beliefs which inspired them and have formed our world.

Various attempts have been made to explain away Constantine's vision. Dancing madonnas are proof that if you stare at anything for long enough your eyes will do odd things. And sometimes you do not even have to stare. Stand in West Berlin and look at the silvery globe of the telecommunications tower in East Berlin and with the sun in the right place you will see a cross of light beaming across the divided city. Constantine is not the only one to have seen a cross over the sun – it is a well documented phenomenon and is quite common, though admittedly Constantine's additional claim of an inscription is not.

Whatever the provenance of Constantine's vision, it had an immediate

Constantine preparing to do battle with his arch enemy, Maxentius, sees a cross of light over the sun — a vision which would change world history

effect. When his army joined battle with Maxentius after the dream, every soldier had a new emblem painted on his shield. Later Constantine's old tutor Lactantius would describe it as the letter X with a loop at the top. This was extraordinary. It meant that a Roman army took to the field and gained victory behind shields bearing a symbol of degradation, a sign of the lowest form of capital punishment which Roman justice could mete out — and the loop on the cross made the message more specific because it was a blend of the cross and the Khi-rho symbol, the first two letters of the Greek name for Christ. Constantine, who had previously been rather keen on Apollo to whom, in spite of his broken nose, he felt he bore a physical resemblance, had chosen as his emblem not just a cross but also the Khi-rho sign — Christian shorthand for Christ. It promised revolution for the Roman empire and for all those who called themselves Christians in the centuries which followed.

To us today the cross is synonymous with Christianity. Before Constantine the early Christians had many symbols — the fish, the anchor, the boat. The cross was part of Constantine's revolution. As Sister Charles

Murray, Lecturer in Historical Theology at Nottingham University, says, there was in a sense no symbolism of the cross before Constantine. The only known possible representation is a graffito in the Hall of the Pages on the Palatine in Rome and it has with it an ass's head. There is a dispute as to whether or not it is a Christian symbol, or whether it is a pagan mockery of the cross. But with Constantine, because the cross became shorthand for victory, the cross is raised to the forefront of Christian representation. Once Constantine establishes the importance of the cross as a victory symbol, it becomes considerably distanced from any notion of the cross as suffering or pain or a sign of contradiction. After that the cross becomes the great symbol of the Christian religion – not so much in the sense of the humiliation of Christ, but in the triumph of Christ.

The triumph of the Cross – an allegory of the revolution of Constantine. The cross is transformed from a painful reminder of the degradation of Calvary to a symbol of victory, toppling the marble effigies of the old gods

Constantine saw Christ not so much as the suffering servant but more as the guarantor of victory, a welcome source of certainty in an uncertain world. The third century, into which Constantine had been born, was a time of martyrdom for Christians and of crisis for the Roman empire. Politics had become more than usually deadly. For as many as twenty-five emperors power brought little more than a premature and bloody death.

Some measure of stability returned with the accession in AD 284 of Diocletian, the keen gardener and unsuccessful persecutor of Christians, but the economy was reeling. There had been massive inflation and widespread bankruptcy. The metal of imperial coins had fallen so far short of their face value that even tax inspectors preferred payment in kind, and this, according to Professor William Frend, Professor Emeritus of Ecclesiastical History at Glasgow University, brings us to an often neglected discipline – the economics of theology.

During the third century, particularly during the second half of the third century, Christianity was the only organisation which was financially stable. The rest of the Roman empire – the towns – was declining; buildings were just patched up. The Church, on the other hand, was a stable and reasonably wealthy organisation and by the end of the third century it was a state within a state. The great persecution failed when its fourth edict ordered all the people to sacrifice to pagan gods – not just the bishops, everybody. There was immediate and impassioned opposition and the opposition won. As Eusebius describes it, the axe grew blunt in the hand of the executioners and they grew desperate as one Christian after another volunteered for martyrdom.

It was a victory of the spirit, and Constantine, though he was in the West, the area least affected by Christianity, had seen the victory of Christianity in the time of Diocletian when he was in the imperial court, and he remembered. The lessons Constantine drew from Diocletian's failure cannot be calculated, but what is documented is that once he became sole emperor, Christianity for the first time found itself being used as a tool of state.

As Professor Averil Cameron, Professor of Late Antique and Byzantine Studies at King's College, London, says, when Constantine decided that he was going to support the Christian Church, he found a very useful instrument there in the bishops. The bishops were organised in a network, they were all ready and waiting. He worked through them. And from the moment he began doing that, Christians had an influence on him. He started preaching sermons to the court on Fridays. All the courtiers had to stand there listening to him and apparently some of them found it rather embarrassing.

But were those Friday sermons simply part of an astute political strategy? Was Constantine a wily politician cynically mobilising Christian supporters or was he an over-enthusiastic believer? Professor Stuart Hall, Professor of Ecclesiastical History at King's College, London, believes that from what Constantine writes he seems to have had a very powerful sense of vocation, which he saw as reinforcing his military skill and his desire for the empire. To understand his views, it is important to realise that the Romans were themselves religious people in an old-fashioned pre-Christian sense. The function of a god was to make the empire prosper. There was no other point in having gods and from Augustus on it was the old-fashioned gods who sustained the peace of the empire. To placate those gods, to please them, was the best way of making sure the empire prospered.

The emperors immediately before Constantine decided, for their own reasons, that their reorganising of the empire needed the destruction of

Christianity. Constantine in his youth had probably observed the martyrs and he was present while the churches were being destroyed. This somehow convinced him that the martyrs were on to the real God and when the real God started tipping Constantine's own enemies into rivers, in the middle of difficult battles, Constantine's convictions grew and grew.

Constantine's was a genuine conviction – albeit one based more on might is right than on the first shall be last. Though still unbaptised, he nevertheless made no secret of his preference for Christianity. His private household was run by deacons. Courtiers were subjected to daily morning prayers as well as to regular lectures against polytheism. The old Roman laws penalising the childless were repealed so that Christians who chose celibacy no longer had to pay extra taxes. To be Christian now was a matter of courting privilege rather than danger. Was there then an immediate rush among the ambitious to become baptised?

Robin Lane Fox, Fellow and Tutor in Ancient History at New College, Oxford, thinks that it was a slow process. There were certainly people who rushed in and they were encouraged by Constantine's mag-nificent support for the Church. He gave the churches everything they had not had before – land, riches, prominent public buildings, legal privileges, support for Christian careers and so forth – so it was very much the bandwagon on which to jump. But people could not jump on and stay on, unless they came to see that there was a particular union of belief and practice, or cult and philosophy, in Christian teaching which had not been present in previous pagan worship. It was much more a religion in our modern sense than pagan worship had been for many people in the empire.

While non-Christians at court were weighing up the pros and cons of baptism, outside the court the message about the emperor's preferences took some time to get through. Professor Averil Cameron says that in the first years of Constantine Christians, particularly clergy, were still being sought out, sometimes thrown into prison, sometimes having their hands or feet cut off, or even being put to death. Then suddenly everything turned upside-down. We can see in contemporary writings Christians' amazement at finding an emperor who for the very first time is on their side. They had to change their entire view of history. The Roman empire had been an enemy for them, and now suddenly, they are part of it. They are the mainstream.

Christianity had been rehabilitated and so too had another influence in Constantine's religious and emotional life – his mother Helena, of whom he was fiercely protective. Sister Charles Murray says that according to St Ambrose Helena was originally a servant girl, born in Turkey, and that she was the concubine of Constantine's father the emperor Constantius

Chlorus. But other sources say she was, in fact, his wife. It is now believed that she was the wife, rather than simply the mistress, of the emperor, but was abandoned for political reasons by him. He married the stepdaughter of another emperor, Maximian, in order to further his career, and it was not until Constantine became emperor that his mother was restored to the dignity he felt she should have always had.

St Helena, the rehabilitated mother of Constantine and the world's first ecclesiastical archaeologist, begins her less than systematic investigations into the whereabouts of the true cross by questioning the Jews of Jerusalem

From then on Helena fared well. Whatever scandal caused Constantine to have his wife and son murdered never touched Helena. And it is Helena, not Constantine, who is recognised as a canonised saint in both the churches of the east and the west. Constantine only makes the grade in the east. Legends have grown round Helena. A confusion over names led to the claim that she was British, the daughter of Old King Cole. Still further flights of fancy have suggested that she was Jewish and that Constantine was a leper. But the truth is stranger than fiction.

In her old age the emperor's mother became the world's first ecclesiastical archaeologist, credited with identifying the sites of the birth, death, resurrection and ascension of Jesus. Less creditably she is blamed for starting the craze for Holy Land relic hunting. It was alleged that she found the True Cross and that she gave two of the sacred nails to Constantine. One he wore in his helmet, the other was part of a bridle for his horse. All this may smack of superstition, rather than of faith. But it is a mistake to think of Constantine's faith in twentieth-century categories. He was convinced by monotheism and convinced by Christ, but his Christianity grew out of a non-Christian background. As Professor Stuart Hall points out, as a young man Constantine had adopted a tradition of the worship of the unconquered sun and he did not discard it completely. He somehow rolled it into his Christianity. There were various ways of doing that. The sun had for a long time been a symbol of the one god in Platonist philosophical theology and various parts of the Bible speak of God as Light or as Sun of Righteousness and Christ himself as the Light of the World. So it was really quite easy for Constantine to transfer himself from a devotion to the unconquered sun to the unconquered Christ who rose from the dead and rescued Constantine's army from defeat.

Religious mixed bathing then as now was the norm. Pagan ideas became Christianised and vice versa. Jesus nailed to the cross was compared to Odysseus strapped to the mast. Clement of Alexandria went so far as to speak of Jesus as the new Orpheus braving Hades for those he loves. With so much change there was a need for continuity and nowhere does this come through more strongly than the contemporary writing of Eusebius of Caesarea the survivor, a bishop, a courtier and a historian – in that order.

Professor Frend says that Eusebius, who was born about 269, became a strong believer in the co-operation of Church and State. He sets out in his *Chronicle* to justify Christianity as the original religion of the human race. And he writes the first eight books of his *Ecclesiastical History* to show that Christianity is not something new but is the traditional religion – right from creation. Eusebius survived persecution and an accusation of heresy. He was fanatically loyal to Constantine and Constantine repaid him by making him his personal adviser.

Christianity now had to face all the temptations of social acceptability, and Sister Charles Murray says there is evidence of the Church standing out against its new imperial patrons. Constantia, who was Constantine's half-sister, asked Eusebius to send her a portrait of Christ. In return, she got a very harsh letter saying that to make a portrait of Christ is against the Christian tradition. To use modern terminology it is heretical to do so, because you cannot portray the divinity. Eusebius was so incensed with Constantia, that he sought out the rumoured portrait and had it destroyed. It is probable his sharp reaction was prompted by a fear that recently acquired Christianity could easily be weakened and revert to a form of idolatry.

But Dr Hilda Davidson, Lecturer in Anglo-Saxon and Norse Studies and Fellow of Lucy Cavendish College, Cambridge, believes that there was no need for such defensiveness. Paganism and Christianity were not in direct equal competition. The whole basis of paganism, she says, was that it was very close to the earth and the local place. But it was not a world religion. It had no sacred books, no features of belief. It had powers and gods and goddesses and supernatural beings and it did not matter whether its followers were virtuous or not – this was not relevant. The pagan religion was concerned with success, rather than with virtue. It did not help very much in great sorrows and in explaining why the world suffers. Among the pagans there must have been many people who lived lives that the Christians would say were good lives, but Christianity opened so many new avenues, that the pagan religion was largely left behind. Perhaps people had grown beyond it. Life had altered and they wanted to go further. The names of all the old gods of the ancient world are still familiar to us today from drama, music and poetry – as familiar as the names of the saints and martyrs of the early church. But why is it that there are no great pagan priests or leaders who have remained as household names? If the devil has all the best tunes, is it true that the Christians have all the best leaders?

Robin Lane Fox says that paganism on the whole was not a religion that needed leaders. It was a religion of accepted practice more than of doctrinaire belief, let alone a system with leaders like bishops, and this is shown very clearly in Christians' and pagans' reactions to each other. When the pagans wished to persecute Christians they learned that they must persecute the top people. When the Christians in turn wished to close down paganism, they did not persecute people so much as destroy places. That is a real difference in the nature of the two religions.

But it was not only a question of lack of leadership. It was also, Dr Hilda Davidson believes, a matter of good timing. In the time of Constantine, she says, people were looking everywhere for something that would make life better because life was very hard. There was a great deal of fighting, killing and wholesale destruction. The future was grim for little farmers, who were in danger of having their throats cut by the latest power-hungry faction. And so everybody was looking round for an answer. People wanted something more, something that covered the bad things in life as well as the good things in life, and something that brought people together.

It was not only orthodox Christianity which answered these emotional and religious needs. There were mystery religions and various saviour cults, exotic earth mothers and, throughout Constantine's lifetime, various forms of Christian Gnosticism. The basic principle of Gnosticism was a reliance on the lure of secret teaching and a dualism which looked down on matter. Dualism was, and indeed is, a system which sees the world as a battleground between the god of goodness and the god of evil, two separate and independent first causes. The god of evil is seen as having the upper hand in the material world. Those who combined Christianity and Gnosticism identified the creating God of the Hebrew Bible as inferior to, and separate from, the God of Love of the New Testament. Some Gnostics were rigorously ascetic; others were deliberately licentious, believing that once in possession of secret teachings, a believer could not be tainted by sin. Gnostics were keen on melons – light-bearing food they believed. Their activities have tended to be written out of official Christian records but they were, according to Professor Henry Chadwick, Regius Professor Emeritus of Divinity and Master of Peterhouse, Cambridge, both energetic and widespread.

The biggest of all Gnostic sects, he explains, was founded in the middle of the third century by a man from Mesopotamia called Mani. He founded the Manichees and they had an active, thrusting missionary programme. Within a hundred years of Mani's death they stretched from Cadiz to Chinese Turkestan. Like ground elder, they spread, though they never became enormously numerous. Manichaeism was the most potent form of Gnosticism. One of its most famous disciples was Augustine of Hippo who was an adherent of ten years. He was so embarrassed about the length of time that afterwards he said it was only nine.

The word Gnosticism is often used much more loosely by many modern historians to describe a religiosity, which professionals call syncretism, in other words you take a stewpot and put everything you can find into it and give it a good stir. The basic presupposition of that religiosity is that all religions are saying the same thing under different names. The myths of Mithras, Attis or of Isis are all in essence revealing the same wisdom, therefore they can all be put in the same pot. Christianity, which is monotheistic and on the whole not very tolerant of other people's myths, was a less than happy ingredient in a syncretistic stewpot, but the Gnostics were willing to stir it into the stew much to the fury of orthodox Christians.

Christian Gnostics held on to their secret teachings but found it hard to accept that Jesus was really man and went through birth, suffering and death. Their doubts were part of a larger debate about the enigma of Jesus – man, god, or god/man – a debate which rocked the Christian community in the second part of Constantine's reign. It was a controversy which came to a head in Alexandria, sparked off by a quarrel between Bishop Alexander and a tall, round-shouldered dockland parish priest called Arius.

Professor Henry Chadwick says that Arius was a very popular figure in the city. He had a great reputation for writing theological sea shanties which the dockers enjoyed singing. He had a great following among the young women of the city. He used to have special services on Wednesdays and Fridays with enormous congregations. He began to feel that there were obstacles between Christians and the educated people of this very intelligent city. It was not quite a university town in our medieval and modern sense, but the atmosphere of questioning and debate was the same. Arius began to feel that orthodox Christianity was too hard to swallow for the parishioners, academics and non-academics in an intellectual and sophisticated city. He wanted to make it easier for them to have faith. Arius himself did not find it at all easy to believe that the transcendent first cause of all creation could have suffered as the incarnate Lord, Jesus Christ. Yes, Jesus was supreme in the order of creation, perhaps beyond the order of creation, but not of one being with his Father. In other words, he was on the human side of the gulf between creator and creature.

The dispute between Arius and Alexander alarmed Constantine. He was sure that dissension was bad for the church. An emperor who allowed dissension to spread unabated might loose the hard-won favour of heaven. So Constantine wrote a letter.

Constantine, emperor, to the bishops of the great Church.

'My beloved brethren — it must be clear to all men that nothing is more important to me than the fear of God. You have already planned to hold a synod at Ancyra in Galatia. Change your plans. Come to Nicea, a city in Bithynia. The Italian and European bishops are coming already. Come to Nicea, it has excellent weather and I myself will be able to take part in and mark your discussions.'

The bishops duly gathered in Nicea to decide what was orthodox belief and what was heresy. But who were they to decide? And why did their deliberations matter? Professor Henry Chadwick says that they were almost all Greek bishops. But, and it is quite a big but, there was a small number, namely five, who came from the West. The bishop of Rome, Sylvester, was told all about it. He did not turn up himself, but he did send two of his presbyters as his legates and he was given great honour in the Council. His legates were given primatial seats in honour of the great dignity of the great church of Peter and Paul and the capital of the empire. And if the two presbyters representing the bishop of Rome were against anything, that was a little like the Transport and General Workers' Union exercising a card veto at the Trades Union Congress. The numbers of representatives from the West was not as significant as who they represented.

Everyone present knew that the assembly of 325 was without precedent. There was a very strong self-consciousness which comes through in the surviving documents of the Council, that nothing like this had ever happened before. No one had ever brought 220 bishops together in one place. Indeed they were so impressed with their own numbers that soon they were talking of 300 being present and then, within twenty-five years, this had become the 318 which is the number of the servants of Abraham in the Book of Genesis, and was a sacred number.

The Council was much bigger than anything anybody had ever seen and the emperor himself presided. He gave them all a great dinner at the end and Constantine's biographer, Eusebius, tells us that though there had been some absenteeism at the Council, there was none at the dinner. The representatives were very conscious that dining with the emperor was symbolic. Previously the churches had been persecuted. There were bishops at Nicea who had lost arms, legs and eyes in the persecution. They came in as heroes who had been through the equivalent of terrible physical torture. They were brave men who had really had a rough time, so that there was a feeling that Christianity was embarking on a completely new way of life – not only surviving but also controlling imperial edicts.

In a way, Nicea was a culmination of the Christian revolution. Not only were Christians no longer outcasts, but more than that, their internal theological disputes were of prime importance and could command the emperor's undivided attention. They had a creed shared throughout the Christian world. The days of hiding were over. Of course there were new pitfalls. Toleration from outside was matched by a new sense of internal intolerance. Then as now Church and State can make uneasy bedfellows.

But why was it that Constantine and thousands of others chose Christianity? Robin Lane Fox says that this is the big question and that there is a simple answer. They believed they were saved. They thought that in the next world, they as Christians would go to a better existence. They felt that Jesus suffered for them and had redeemed them and that the teaching as presented in the Gospels, which were a narrative of Jesus' life, were true, certain and beyond doubt, that its picture of how God cared for the world and sent his only Son and had redeemed it from sin and error was entirely convincing.

They also admired, and indeed pagan critics too admired, Christianity's ethical aspirations when best put into practice – a religion of gentleness, of humility, of charity, of real respect for the poor in whom spiritual merit resided. This was not something characteristic of pagan society; pagans tended more towards philanthropy than charity. There were all the other attractions of Christianity. It was intellectually alive. The heresies were fascinating, divisive, passionately argued. There was scope for enormous excitement and intellectual effort in trying to define questions of almost impossible definition. At the same time the prominence of Christian buildings, careers, Christian riches in the world had attractions for individuals who either wished to receive them, to dispense them or to dominate them. And Christianity offered scope for people who were prepared to try to be perfect and had a practical regime for impractical goodness in the model of the Gospel sayings. There was scope for an outstanding effort, either as a saint in the desert or even as a celibate lady. You might go into a special community from an early age. Christianity could win the heart. It appealed to people's common sense of humanity with their fellow men which had not been eroded by existence under the Roman empire. It offered a tremendous intellectual scope, it offered worldly career scope, and it offered scope for excessive over-achievement. It is no surprise that Christianity emerged as victorious, once it received official backing. It had so much that was just in suspension or in embryo in pagan religious consciousness, and it presented it in a much clearer, firmer package which was irresistible.

The uncomfortable question has to be asked – was then Constantine's Council at Nicea a backward step, an imperial sledgehammer to crack a harmless religious nut? Or was Nicea essential for the survival of the Church? Professor Henry Chadwick believes this is a delicate, exposed nerve of Christian theology. This point is central to understanding the Arian controversy: human beings worship things that they themselves do not completely understand. If we can understand what we worship, then it suddenly ceases to be an object of worship. Human beings can only worship the incomprehensible, that of which we can hardly speak at all, something that is too deep for words. There is a real sense in which the orthodox defence that Jesus was fully God and fully man, at Nicea and later, was defending this incomprehensibility, as the theologians say, of God, the fact that you cannot get your fingers round him, and get him in your fist, and say, I have it. The Arians were a little inclined to think that they had it. They perhaps like some of us today were a little inclined to say, we have mastered logic and we think we can get God underneath our logical rules. The orthodox said you can do nothing of the kind and you never will.

The debate about Jesus' full humanity and full divinity was of the greatest importance. To say that the Redeemer is not on the creator's side of the gulf separating the creator from the creation, which is quite a strong element in Biblical doctrine, does in the long run have knock-on effects on the way you think about the possibility or nature of salvation. In principle that is the doctrine of the Council of Nicea, which is still proclaimed in the Nicene Creed of eucharistic liturgy, so it has remained binding in mainstream Christianity today. Nicea is still a live issue. When the German American theologian, Paul Tillich, published his systematic theology, a distinguished theologian of the Church of England described his position as Arianism with its mythology brought up to date. He was criticised on just that ground, that he had weakened the adherence to the Council of Nicea. When the Vatican expressed dissent from the opinions of Hans Küng, whom everybody admires as a writer, one of their grounds for expressing dissent from his view was that he was a little wobbly on the Nicene Creed.

Although Constantine presided over the Council of Nicea and preached sermons to his courtiers, he remained unbaptised until five weeks before his death. Why the delay? Caution? Hypocrisy? Doubt? Professor Averil Cameron thinks there might have been several reasons. One might be that it would have been going a bit further politically than he was prepared to do at an earlier stage, but more likely the reason was a personal one. People did at that time defer baptism because they felt that once you were baptised you should not commit any more sins. If you did, you risked your immortal soul, and so you deferred baptism until as late as possible so that you went to heaven as pure as you could. So Constantine's late baptism could be seen as a sign of excessive reverence for the ideals of the Christian life.

But it has to be said, Constantine kept the title of High Priest. Right at the end of his reign, he allowed a new temple to be built in Italy to the imperial cult and the worship of his own family. Does that mean that he was hypocritical? The answer, says Professor Cameron, is no. He was in the hot seat, he had to do what was necessary for the state. He had to take political actions, he could not simply change everything overnight.

So Constantine spent only the last few weeks of his life as a baptised Christian. Throughout his life he had always been fond of rich imperial gold and purple, but from his baptism until his death he wore the simple white of a newly baptised convert. He had brought the Church out of the shadows into the centre of government. It was a worldly success, but was it a spiritual mixed blessing? Professor Stuart Hall believes it could be said that the Church consisted of saints before Constantine and of sinners afterwards and that this led to the rise of monasticism. The great surge into monastic life among serious Christians certainly occurred in Constantine's reign and continued in the reign of his sons. One or two modern writers have argued that the revolutionary impact of Christianity, reversing human morality, reversing human institutions, so that love would prevail, was transformed when Constantine made the cross of shame into a military

The baptism of Constantine. Although a convinced Christian, Constantine remained unbaptised until the last five weeks of his life. The delay was not caused by doubt. It was an admission of a problem which is still alive today – the conflict between the practicalities of political power and the ideals of faith

emblem and that this was a complete disaster and a failure. But Professor Hall does not take that view himself. He thinks we should try and look at it from the point of responsibility of government. Constantine thought that responsible government for one who was called by the one God meant promoting the worship of the one God. In fact, he was terrified of the consequences of not doing this. This meant that there were some rather curious consequences of his policy, like rich people all becoming clergy because of tax concessions, a policy which he had to reverse. The bishop of Rome had a palace in Rome which had belonged to Constantine's wife, and so the Christian Church began to go down the road towards institutionalisation. The underdogs and rebels were now not only legalised but their leaders could expect the trappings of worldly power. But this was not necessarily a bad thing. Human beings live in institutions, and these need sanctifying too.

Constantine may indeed have institutionalised Christianity but he had also genuinely tried to bring the humaneness of Christ's teachings into the secular world. He had outlawed crucifixion, forbidden face branding on the grounds that all men, slaves and criminals included, are made in the image of God. He attempted to stop the exposure of infants by making the imperial privy purse liable for the upkeep of children whose fathers could not support them. He outlawed gladiatorial combat and did away with a master's right to torture or kill slaves. He made Sunday a public holiday. All in all an enormous contribution to the Christian revolution. Robin Lane Fox thinks that recently historians have sometimes minimised it in two ways. First they have presented paganism as a system dying under its own weight and essentially commanding little allegiance from the vast majority of the Roman empire's inhabitants by a hundred years before Constantine. That now is an increasingly implausible view. And secondly they have assumed as a corollary that the Christians were already in a comfortable majority by the time that Constantine put his material support behind the faith.

The process of Christian conversion and the gaining of a majority is a slow process after Constantine and the effect of those conversions and the winning of that majority is a real revolution in everything from private life, sexual ideals, matrimonial ideals, attitudes to life in the household and the home, to much wider notions of sin, heresy, false belief, and the devil. These ideas were to hang over Western civilisation for the next 1500 years – all of them fundamentally alien to the pagan belief which had dominated the empire before Constantine saw his cross of light.

THE JEROME CONUNDRUM

Nearly fifty years after the body of the newly baptised emperor Constantine had been laid to rest, as he had requested, in the thirteenth tomb in the Church of the Apostles in Constantinople, a middle-aged scholar with weak eyes, a vicious tongue, and an apocryphal reputation for being good with lions, wrote a letter to a young woman who had become his star pupil. In it he told her about a nightmare he could not forget.

When I decided that I would give up the things of this world, I found I could do without most of my material possessions — but there was one exception. I could not, try as I might, wean myself away from my small library – a collection of books I had bought and even copied myself by hand since my student days. However much I did penance, however much I fasted and prayed, I always ended up creeping back to Cicero or Plautus. Even if I suddenly pulled myself together and read the Bible instead I would close it again, repelled by its clumsiness. Then in the middle of Lent I fell into a fever and everyone thought I was going to die. Instead I dreamt. I was swept up in the spirit and found myself before some sort of tribunal. My eyes were dazzled by a blinding light. There was a judge who spoke to me and asked me what I was. I said, ‘A Christian,’ but he replied, ‘You are a liar. You belong to Cicero, not Christ, for where your treasure is, there your heart is.’

The dreamer was Jerome, a God-haunted man from what we would think of as Yugoslavia and he would have thought of as north-eastern Italy. When the emperor Constantine had his vision of a cross over the sun he had wondered what it meant. Jerome had no such doubts about his dream. In his nightmare he promised the judge whom he interpreted as Christ that he would never possess or even read a non-Christian book again. When he woke he considered himself bound by that oath and only relaxed it in extreme old age when he opened a free school for local children.

In many ways Jerome was a beneficiary of the Constantinian legacy. Because he had been born round about the time of the emperor's death, it was perfectly possible for Jerome as a Christian scholar to move round the countries of the Mediterranean without ever facing the danger of persecution. Indeed, Jerome's life story reads like a gazetteer of the fourth-century world: Rome, Trier, Athens, Bithynia, Antioch, Syria, Constantinople, Jerusalem, and finally Bethlehem. His preoccupations and guilts are those of a Christian trying to come to terms with security. Martyrdom was no longer available – only the slow martyrdom of asceticism. Jerome's main worry was not the threat of paganism as an alternative set of beliefs. What terrified him to the point of fanaticism was the prospect of a Christianity diluted by the urbane culture of the classical world for which he still hankered with every atom of his being.

Later generations would revere Jerome as one of the four great doctors of the Church, along with Augustine, Ambrose, and Gregory the

St Jerome the scholar, painted by Georges de la Tour. He is surrounded by the tools of the religious scholar's trade – a volume of scripture for enlightenment and a human skull, a reminder of the frailty of man no matter how clever

Great. To his contemporaries he was a walking conundrum, eager to love, ready to hate. He was suspected of magic because he could read silently without moving his lips. At one stage he was accused of inducing pious anorexia in a daughter of one of his friends and was drummed out of Rome. Many regarded him as self-centred, misguided, and ambitious. Yet his obsessions, his achievements, and his mistakes still influence every layer of twentieth-century Christian life from attitudes towards sexual behaviour to the way Christian academics approach the Bible. The story of Jerome has cast a long and contorted shadow over the history of Christianity. But can we be sure it bears any relation to Jerome the man?

How much do we really know about the historical Hieronymus the son of Eusebius of Stridon? Professor Henry Chadwick believes that the honest answer is much too much. We have an enormous amount of what he wrote, and his writings, especially his incomparably written letters, are a self-revelation of the kind of a man Jerome was. Those who have lived and worked in universities will all recognise somebody very like St Jerome – the kind of person who is very prickly and defensive with contemporaries or equals and infinitely generous to young students whom he is willing to encourage, patronise and get on the right road. Jerome had a great dread of his own sexual drive. Yet no letters are more remarkable than the ones he wrote to young women who wanted to pursue theology or the ascetic life. They are written with great generosity, but there are two written with the kind of fanaticism which got him a terrible reputation in his own lifetime and some harsh judgements ever since.

Nevertheless, those troublesome letters on sex and marriage proved highly influential. Jerome is often caricatured as a classic case of repressed sexuality. True, he believed that virginity, celibacy, or abstention from sex in marriage were the highest callings a Christian could aspire to. But to make sense of Jerome it is essential to grasp that his beliefs sprang from positive as well as from negative convictions.

In the fourth century, virginity was for the first time becoming respectable. Jerome and many others were teaching that this life was only a precursor to an eternal present. There was no need to attract husbands or wives or to father or mother dynasties, no need to lay down riches for future generations. All that mattered for the individual believer, whether male or female, was to imitate Christ in this world before joining him in heaven. Gratification of any of the senses could be spiritually lethal.

Jerome told young female adherents that they must keep their bodies pale and hungry. To Jerome, health was a sign of worldliness. He has been described both as a madman and as a monster. He certainly had a profound distaste for himself and particularly for his own body. And with due cause. Dr John Kelly, Honorary Fellow of St Edmund Hall, Oxford, says that Jerome was not very much to look at. He is always talking about his miserable body – his corpusculum – and how weak he is. He recalls how he went once to the Acropolis in Athens and was shown there a weight-lifting device for testing athletes. He could not even move it. On the other hand, he had an extraordinary passion for good food and he found that when he took up an ascetic life this was the thing he missed most. He loved gorging himself with rich food.

Dr Kelly says we see him as a monster because we study him with hindsight. But if we had lived along with him he would not necessarily have seemed monstrous. He was a very dazzling man, a very witty man, and he had a magnetic quality. He must have been very charismatic for he fascinated women and he brought a number of men under his spell.

Jerome was fully caught up in the whirlwind of theological argument which racked the Christian community. Tensions were beginning to develop between the East and the West over the nature of the Trinity, the role of divine grace, and the pre-eminence of virginity. Jerome weighed into the fray, monstrosity well to the fore.

Professor Gordon Davies, Professor Emeritus of Theology at Birmingham University, says that Jerome was petty, vindictive, impetuous, spiteful, and lacking in balance. He was a great satirist but he could also be very coarse and we have the evidence from his own hand to prove it. One of the people he did not like was Jovinian, who had apparently been teaching that virginity and marriage were of equal status – one is not better than the other. Now that was quite contrary to the ideals of Jerome, who believed that virginity was the ideal. In fact, he so much despised marriage that he said that Peter's martyrdom could not wash away the defilement of his marriage. Jerome attacked Jovinian for his ideas in a treatise published in 392, and ends up by recording his death. Jovinian, he says, belched out rather than breathed out his life among swine, flesh, and peasants – a nice turn of phrase, but scarcely the charity which is supposed to characterise Christians.

Jovinian was by no means the only person to feel the sharpness of Jerome's pen. Jerome was undoubtedly anti-Semitic. The Jews, he wrote in a treatise on Leviticus, were like single-hoofed, unclean animals, whereas Christians who stood on the Old and New Testaments were cloven-hoofed and therefore clean. He also attacked Pelagius, the British monk, as a corpulent dog puffed up by Scottish porridge. These are selective quotations but, according to Professor Henry Chadwick, present quite a fair picture of Jerome's style.

Jerome was a very difficult man to please. He wrote a commentary on the Epistle to the Galatians in which he followed, as he very often did,

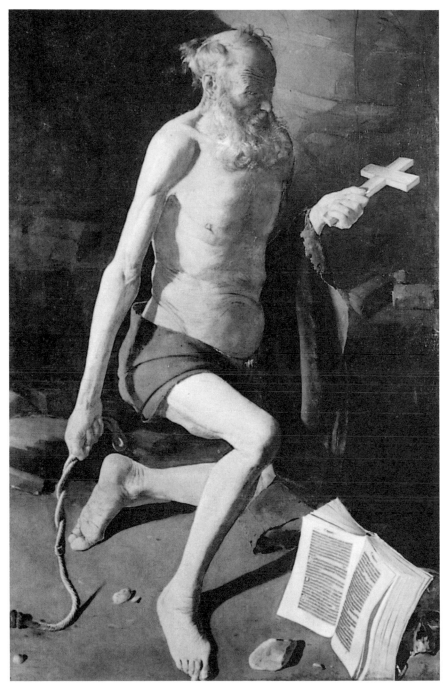

St Jerome, again by de la Tour but this time shown as an ascetic penitent, meditating on the cross and the scriptures and struggling to subdue his emaciated body with the whip

Origen, the Greek theologian of the third century, and said that the quarrel between St Peter and St Paul at Antioch, described in the second chapter of that letter, could not possibly have been a real quarrel, it was an edifying bit of play acting. A copy of this reached Augustine at Hippo. Augustine thought this was a terrible thing to say – it discredited the authority of the Apostles that they should deceive people by play acting – and he wrote to Jerome expostulating and asking him to change this in his commentary. Jerome was extremely offended and eventually sent the letter back three years or so later saying, I think you had better know of an impertinent forgery circulating in your name.

However much the cut and thrust of academic debate occupied Jerome there was another attraction which dominated his life – the lure of the desert. That, he was sure, was where the real spiritual athletes were to be found. He writes with a heartfelt admiration which sounds almost like envy about Bonosus, his childhood friend, who had opted for seeking God on a small barren rock in the Adriatic. Inevitably Jerome turned to the East and towards the desert, but he was not a natural hermit. Professor Henry Chadwick says that Jerome had a very disturbed adolescence, and when he eventually moved to Syria, where he tried being a hermit, he undertook the study of Hebrew because in his cell he was tormented by the memories of the strip shows that he had imprudently been to watch when he was a young man. He found that the study of Hebrew was about the only way in which he could keep his mind in order, and he became a good Hebraist.

In the end this would prove to be far more than an efficient mental discipline. Jerome's desert retreat was in the region of Chalcis in northern Syria – an area crawling with hermits. These were mainly uneducated men who would live alone in caves, up poles, or in ditches. They would meet on Saturdays and Sundays to worship together. They lived in holy and abject squalor.

Jerome was not a normal run-of-the-mill desert hermit. Dr Kelly says that when he took himself into the desert, it was a very unusual retreat. A great contemporary of his, John Chrysostom, retired into the desert in Syria, and lived in almost complete isolation, in great simplicity, literally lying on the rock and creeping into his cave. But Jerome seems to have had quite a decent set-up. He was in touch with his rich grandee friends in Antioch, who brought him his letters week by week. He also had three or four young boy secretaries who took down his dictation, and a whole library of books, so he was not entirely cut off from the world of ideas.

But his desert experiment was not a total success. At first he was overcome by the holy simplicity and the material poverty of his fellow hermits. Then slowly, disillusionment set in. The Syrian desert monks found this strange Westerner with his books, letters and friends highly suspect. And Jerome found there were ecclesiastical politics even in the desert. Trinitarian differences between East and West and Jerome's own inability to keep quiet meant that friction was inevitable. After only three years, a mere grain of sand in the life of most hermits, Jerome returned to city life – first to Antioch, and then to Rome where Damasus was pope.

Damasus, known as the ladies' ear tickler because of his popularity with women, had come to power in an unusually colourful way. As Dr John Matthews, Fellow and Praelector in Ancient History at Queen's College, Oxford, explains, there were two factions for the episcopates – the faction of Ursinus and the faction of Damasus. The election was disputed and the supporters of Damasus set about their opponents in one of the great churches of Rome and left 137 of them dead on the floor. That is the description given by a contemporary pagan historian, Ammianus Marcellinus. A Christian source puts the number of deaths higher. Probably both figures are correct because more people died later of injuries. One hundred and thirty-seven people were left dead on the floor; thirty or forty died later.

Ammianus said who would not fight for a prize which brought so many rewards. By way of explanation he added that the bishops of Rome could eat dinners fit for kings, dine with matrons, parade round the city in gorgeous clothes, and in general exercise tremendous secular influences as metropolitan prelates. Some were scandalised. Others thought that this was a due reward for the Church's efforts in the fourth century. Damasus is known as a relatively worldly prelate. He acquired more secular power than other popes had done. He also did much more than other popes before him, to build up the position of the Church in Rome by building churches, making the Church a visual presence in the streets of the city. That process too had been begun by Constantine.

The Christian community in Rome to which Jerome returned in 382 was far from edifying. The street fighting had stopped but comfort and materialism had seeped into the lives of the clergy and the laity. Jerome railed against the vanity of finely-dressed priests who delighted only in distributing gossip and receiving gifts. During the desert years, Damasus was one of the many people Jerome had written to without ever receiving a reply. But once in Rome Jerome succeeded in impressing Damasus – now an old man. And it is the ear tickler who set Jerome on the road to his greatest achievement.

That achievement, says Dr Kelly, owed its origin to Damasus noticing Jerome. Damasus rather valued this very talented and very deferential younger man. Jerome knew how to be deferential when it suited him.

The pope asked him to make certain revisions to the Bible translations because he was not satisfied with the rather rough Latin translations of the Bible which were current in the West. So Jerome started translating. Satisfied with his work Damasus commissioned him to make a complete translation of the Bible. Jerome, being a fine scholar with a very good scholarly instinct, realised that you could not just translate the old Latin into fresh and modern Latin, or even translate the Greek of the Old Testament or of the New Testament into new Latin. With the Old Testament it dawned on him gradually, but blindingly, that he had to go back to the Hebrew, his desert lifeline.

That blinding realisation scandalised others. By going back to the original sources, Jerome was merely doing what any modern scholar would do. To a fourth-century mind, Jerome was treading on the toes of inspiration. As Professor Gordon Davies explains, the Septuagint, that is to say the Old Testament in Greek, was believed to have been inspired translation. St Augustine for example had a long correspondence with Jerome on this very subject. Augustine thought it was quite wrong to go back to the Hebrew. He was eventually persuaded to the contrary but it took a long time. At the same time as translating, Jerome produced commentaries on the books of the Old Testament. These had a great vogue and were spread all over the Mediterranean world. Gradually his reputation as a biblical scholar increased.

While Jerome was engaged in this great work of biblical scholarship, other elements of Christian practice were falling into place. In Jerusalem, Cyril, its much exiled bishop, was devising forms of liturgy which would ensure that Christian worship was accessible through the emotions as well as through the intellect. As Father Edward Yarnold SJ, Tutor in Theology at Campion Hall, Oxford, explains, what Cyril did first of all was to work out a series of what we would call Holy Week Services for all the worshippers so that they would actually walk round the holy sites to celebrate the sacred days of Holy Week and the death and resurrection of Christ. On Maundy Thursday, for example, they would go up to the Mount of Olives, to the Church of the Ascension, and they would come down in procession to the bottom of the valley, the Garden of Olives. Lamenting there, they would join in the spirit and agony in the Garden of Gethsemane. Then they would have an all-night vigil and end up in the church for Good Friday where they would pray under the Cross.

There still survives one wonderful set of Cyril's sermons connected with baptism. In them he says the believer can never weary of hearing of the Passion, especially in the holy places. Others, he says, can only hear, but those lucky enough to be present in Jerusalem can also see and feel. It is this attempt to try to get people seeing and feeling the events of the

Passion and resurrection of Christ that marks Cyril out as an innovator. Undoubtedly Cyril derived some of his ideas from the pagan mystery religions, which also had a liturgy which aimed to get the people to enter into the feelings of the god or goddess they were honouring.

St Cyril (315–386), Jerusalem's much exiled bishop, who believed that Christian worship should appeal to the emotions as well as to the intellect

It was in Jerome's world that pilgrimage really became popular, largely because the passing of persecution meant that Christians had to face no more dangers than any other travellers. Martyria, or shrines, were built wherever holy people had died. The Holy Land itself soon became pock-marked with pilgrim sites. And there were other goals of pilgrimage too – Rome, Antioch, Constantinople. Even the desert monks became tourist attractions with enthusiastic pilgrims going out into the Syrian wastelands to count how many times Simeon Stylites genuflected on top of his columns.

We have first-hand knowledge of the enthusiasm with which fourth-century Christians tackled pilgrimage from the diary of Egeria the travelling nun, addressed to her sisters in Spain or France. But is it a picture of faith or of naivety? Dr John Wilkinson, Canon of St George's, Jerusalem, does not think she was naive. There are two ways of searching for what she intended to do: one is the letter of Valerius, and the other what one can read into Egeria's own account of her travels. Valerius was very nearly right. He said that in search of God's grace, Egeria read the Bible and then set off to explore the countryside. Where he was wrong was where he says that Egeria was very fatigued by all this travelling and that the fatigue was actually part of her merit. Egeria does not say that at all.

She says she is tired, but she does not make an issue of her tiredness. What Egeria wanted to do when she set off from Spain or Constantinople was to undertake a voluntary act of pilgrimage. She went to the Holy Land to approach God.

But was Egeria's search substantially different from the pagan awareness of the holiness of some particular places, reverence for the genius loci? Is there anything which marks out Egeria's experience as different? Dr David Hunt, Lecturer in Classics at Durham University, thinks that there is an underlying sense of having gained a great deal spiritually. One of Egeria's favourite words is *desiderium*, the Latin word for longing. She had this tremendous longing for these places and she talks about this longing driving her up to the top of Mount Sinai and to the top of Mount Nebo, even getting off her donkey and clambering up on foot – not the sort of thing the Roman world went in for. She knew there was something to be gained spiritually from all this. It is not enough just to be at the holy spot; pilgrimage carries greater rewards than that.

Although he did not realise it at the time, when Jerome received his great biblical commission from Pope Damasus his days in Rome were already numbered. He was about to go on enforced pilgrimage. Damasus died and Jerome found himself without a protector. He was more or less run out of the city. Some have put this down to thwarted papal ambitions. The truth is probably less simple. While in Rome, Jerome had achieved some success and not a little notoriety as an adviser to various wealthy pious women, including Marcella, Adella, Lea, Felicitas and Marcellina. He had a profound influence over these women – coaching them towards new feats of asceticism. But he was influenced as well as influencing – particularly by a widow called Paula who never took a bath unless she was seriously ill.

Paula was a wealthy Roman matron, a committed Christian. She had a daughter called Eustochium, and according to Sister Charles Murray Jerome undertook a cross between the spiritual direction of this girl and an attempt to organise a Christian women's religious group. We know about it simply because the letters he wrote to them survive. Eustochium was the recipient of Jerome's letter about his nightmare and she became his favourite student. She studied the Bible, learnt enough Hebrew to be able to chant the Psalms and to Jerome's delight was determined to spend her life as a consecrated virgin. Her sister, Blesilla, would prove more of a problem. Much to Jerome's displeasure she had married. When her husband died, she embraced asceticism with a convert's zeal. She fasted herself to death.

Naturally this caused a scandal which was then exacerbated by the public knowledge that Paula had fainted at Blesilla's funeral. Jerome was seen as a pariah encouraging wealthy women to mortify themselves to the point of death. His previous readiness to condemn all the weaknesses of the Church in Rome meant he had few friends among the clergy. A formal enquiry was held. We do not know its conclusions, but immediately afterwards Jerome left Rome for good and set off for the Holy Land. He was soon joined by Paula, Eustochium, and their friends. After much travelling round the pilgrim sites they all settled in Bethlehem.

As Professor Gordon Davies explains, there were two establishments set up near the Church of Nativity – one was a monastery for men, looked after by Jerome, and the other was a nunnery, looked after by Paula. Jerome had an immense number of visitors, who came to seek his advice, on top of which he had a great number of letters from all over the civilised world asking how to interpret a particular passage from scripture. Far from being in retreat, he became a very busy man.

From the time of his exile Jerome had remarkably little time for Ambrose, the suave bishop of Milan. Dr Matthews thinks he knows why Jerome hated Ambrose. It is possible that when Jerome left Rome in 385 he believed that Ambrose had had a part in the ecclesiastical commission which invited him to leave. Ever after that, Jerome always described Ambrose in, at best, ambiguous – if not in very hostile – terms as a politician and also as a scholar. He criticised Ambrose's scholarship in a no-holds-barred way. This was possible because, like Damasus, Ambrose had more secular than ecclesiastical qualifications at the time of his election. Ambrose had been governor of the province of Aemilia–Liguria, the North Italian province which included Milan and Turin. In 374 when bishop Auxentius of Milan died, Ambrose intervened in the episcopal contest and was made bishop himself.

Ambrose came from a political family background of administrators and important men in the state. He brought to the city of Milan more practical experience than ecclesiastical understanding. Inevitably his first years in the episcopate were theologically ill-informed. The Christians of Milan had to set in hand his theological training because when he was acclaimed as bishop he had only the rudimentary knowledge needed as preparation for baptism. However, within ten years he had made himself one of the leading Latin fathers, which is no mean achievement.

Ambrose's secular career smacked of dangerously worldly success to Jerome, who was now installed as the presiding father figure over the Bethlehem monasteries – although he fought shy of the title abbot. In many ways Jerome's world was coming to an end. As the fourth century spills into the fifth a barbarian foe who could not be deflected by sharp words or vehemence of faith was waiting in the wings. As Dr David Hunt explains, a number of the pilgrims who flocked to the holy places, particularly in the early fifth century, were refugees from the increasing barbarian raids in the West. In the later part of his life, Jerome talks about his monastery in Bethlehem being besieged by people who are fleeing from the ravages of their estates in the West. He is diverted from his

St Ambrose (340–397). Together with St Augustine and St Gregory the Great, he and Jerome would come to be venerated as the four doctors of the Church.

scholarly work on his biblical translation through having to attend to the needs of people bereft of everything but their faith. In his old age Jerome was sure civilisation was about to topple.

More personal anguish was to follow. In 404 Paula died. Jerome was devastated. 'She who was the consolation and support of my life has died – the world is empty,' he wrote. Eustochium took over the running of Paula's monastic community in Bethlehem. It had now grown to fifty nuns. For the rest of his life Eustochium would be Jerome's mainstay. He was heartbroken by her death in 419. One year later he died and was buried near Paula and Eustochium beneath the floor of the Church of the Nativity.

What had Jerome achieved? Professor Gordon Davies thinks that Christianity would have been a little different without him. His support of the monastic ideal – of celibacy, of virginity – was such that the monastic movement took off. By the year 400, owing not a little to his efforts, monasticism was regarded by many as the ideal and it was going to dominate the whole of the medieval outlook.

There has always been an ascetic strand in Christian thought, stemming from the Gospel injunction if any man would come after me, let him deny himself, and take up his cross and follow me. The idea of self-denial is part of Christian discipleship from its earliest days. Then, at the end of the second century AD, the idea that the body is in some sense, if not evil, at least highly regrettable, passes into Christian thought from Greek philosophy. Plato said that the body is the tomb of the soul. Christians did not go as far as Mani – who thought that the body was evil and that matter was evil – but they began to consider that there was a continual battle between the body and the soul in which, to attain salvation, the spirit must triumph over the body. So asceticism of a puritanical kind, which Professor Gordon Davies believes is somewhat contrary to the real nature of Christianity, as expressed in the New Testament, became the goal for every individual. And that is, in part, the work of Jerome. But is it a misunderstanding of the Biblical interpretation of human nature, where the body and the spiritual side of human beings are indissolubly linked? After all, as C. S. Lewis said, God likes matter – he created it.

Jerome's conviction that virginity and celibacy were best, which he had championed throughout his long working life, would have far-reaching consequences, not only for the Church but also for the world. Dr Matthews says that some people have thought that the Church undermined the Empire in various ways. One of them was (and this is Gibbon's view) that it diverted people's commitments from a secular to an ecclesi astical, or other-worldly context. It distracted them from the problems of the temporal world and made them waste their energies in foolish speculation – in Gibbon's opinion – about theology. They would have been better advised to have thought about their cities rather than their churches. Other people have thought that the Church attracted recruits who would otherwise have served in administration and government. For example, there is no telling what Ambrose of Milan would have become if he had stayed in government. And there is Augustine of Hippo, who was converted in Milan in the mid-380s when he held a post as Professor of Rhetoric in the city and was thinking of becoming a governor himself. There are many other people, bishops such as Basil of Caesarea, and Gregory of Nazianzus, famous figures of the fourth-century Church who might have been secular potentates.

But of course it had to be said in defence of the Church that secular bureaucracy had a great way, and the Roman bureaucracy certainly had, of nullifying talent. A man like Ambrose could have become a provincial governor and a bureaucrat and we might have heard no more of him. The Church gave people great chances to express themselves that they would not have had in the government. Such men made a better contribution to the Church than they could have done to the State. Cities came to cluster round their church, and to find loyalties in their church. It is possible to argue that the Church, far from damaging city patriotism, enhanced it.

In spite of all Jerome's prejudices and extremism, Dr John Kelly believes that he enhanced the life of the Church in his day and was in some sense a bridge builder. And he left a legacy to Christians of the future which was far more important than the sharpness of his tongue. Here was a very prominent Westerner who had come to settle in Bethlehem and spent many years there.

Jerome also gave Europe his translation of the Bible, known as the Vulgate, one of the greatest and most influential works ever written. In Britain much is made of the Authorised Version of the Bible, composed by a committee of people, as one of the greatest and most influential treasures that the seventeenth century has bequeathed to the English-speaking world. How much greater was the treasure which Jerome in the Vulgate bequeathed to the whole of Western civilisation.

But Jerome achieved more than that. Although he was not an original thinker, he was a marvellous exponent of agreed doctrine and he was able to put out in a very forceful and convincing way what you might call the straight-up-and-down Catholic doctrine. At the same time he was able to infuse it with an immense spirituality because he was a terribly devout man. He had this wonderful and simple devotion to the child Jesus and this Jesus-centred worship radiates from all his writings. He was certainly a profound ascetic of the kind which most people do not like these days, but perhaps we are the worse for not having a streak of that ourselves.

Jerome's dream of being judged more a Ciceronian than a Christian belonged firmly to the world of nightmare. Professor Henry Chadwick believes it holds the key to his most lasting achievement. The two great things that Jerome did for Christianity, he says, were, first, the fostering of asceticism by reconciling it with a positive humanism. That cost Jerome a lot of blood to achieve. He had been educated extremely well. He knew Virgil by heart, as did Augustine. If all the manuscripts of Virgil had been lost, they could have reconstructed all of them. So that reconciliation of asceticism with high culture and literature was one thing that Jerome had achieved. The other, which is not unrelated, and in fact is almost an aspect of the first, was his translation of the Bible. In this way Jerome made it easier for people of high culture to read the Bible without dropping it because the translation of the old Latin missionaries was so awful. In the West his translation gradually became more and more widely diffused. It became the Bible of the medieval Catholic Church and it has remained predominantly the Bible of the Roman Catholic Church to this day. It differed from the Bible of the Greek Church since, though the Greek Church had the Bible in Greek, it had an inferior Bible text to the one Jerome had used. This is one of the paradoxes of the sixteenth-century Renaissance and Reformation of Erasmus and Luther. They wanted to get back to the Greek Bible, to the sources, but in point of fact, the Bible that the Renaissance and the Reformation got back to was what we call the received text – the Bible of the Greek churches of the late medieval period. As a witness to the original of what the Apostles wrote, Jerome's Latin Vulgate was a superior witness, more ancient and based on a very good manuscript tradition. Jerome's Vulgate frequently preserves the original text against the late medieval manuscripts. Today it is still treated by scholars as a most important witness, always to be weighed with great respect. The puny, god-fearing man from Yugoslavia, most criticised and much criticising, still influences the thought, spirituality and practice of the Christian Church.

THE LION OF ROME

There is a story, most probably true at heart, if not in detail, that Attila the squat, the thinly-bearded Hun, known to later generations as the scourge of God, was stopped in his Romeward tracks and persuaded to retreat by the words of the middle-aged bishop of that threatened city who met him south of Lake Garda in the year 452. So much is attested

Leo I, bishop of Rome from 440 461, shown wearing the papal tiara and with a full complement of fingers. He came to be credited with, or blamed for, laying the foundations of the medieval papacy

Attila the Hun, the scourge of God, a war lord known for his penetrating gaze and his preference for clean clothes

by contemporary sources. Subsequent more fanciful historians have improved upon the account. Two hundred years after the event, Paul the deacon suggested that Attila turned tail not because of papal eloquence but because of an apostolic henchman visible to him alone.

> *After the Pope had left, Attila was asked by his men why he had shown such out of character deference and why he had agreed to do almost everything the Pope had asked. Attila replied he had not been cowed by the pope who had just spoken to him but he had been much more in awe of that other man — the one with white hair and a much more distinguished bearing, dressed in priestly vestments and standing at the pope's elbow. The silent but fierce old man held an unsheathed sword which Attila knew threatened death if the Pope's petition was ignored.*

The pope in question was an Italian of Etruscan origin called Leo, the first bishop of Rome whose writings still survive. Paul the Deacon did not identify Leo's sword-wielding companion. He did not need to.

By the end of Leo's reign all Christendom knew that wherever the bishop of Rome was, Peter the fisherman, the first and fieriest of the apostles, was not far behind.

Leo, by all accounts a gentle man, although with little time for sunworshippers or for priests engaged in usury, dominated his century. His convictions so strengthened the Church in Rome that a role reversal took place which is still in force today. Before Leo, the Church in Rome drew prestige from the international standing of the city in which it was based. After Leo, Rome as a city was politically a spent force; any glory she would have in the future would be by courtesy of the Church she once persecuted.

Leo's certainty, so needed in his own age, casts a long shadow. He is credited or accused of laying the foundation of the medieval papacy. His insistence on the primacy of Peter has unified and divided the Church. His theology on the virgin birth and the incarnation still forms the minds of the vast majority of Christians today.

Leo was born into a world which was crumbling. In the early years of the fifth century the unthinkable had happened – barbarian hordes had crossed the Rhine. It is probable that in the very early years of Leo's life his family migrated south to Rome in the wake of the Gothic incursions. Leo would have been no more than a child when Alaric the Visigoth took Rome for three humiliating days. On hearing the news, old St Jerome, sitting in Bethlehem, wept for a fallen city and predicted the end of the world he had known. Professor Robert Browning, Emeritus Professor of the University of London, understands why. If you were a Martian on a spaceship observing earth in the course of the fifth century, he says, the great event that you would see would be the disintegration of the Roman Empire which had been there with more or less the same territorial boundaries for 500 years. By the end of that century, Britain, France, Spain, Italy and North Africa from the Atlantic to the middle of what is now Libya, were all under the control of Germanic states.

As a young man Leo would have been reminded time and again that the things of this world are transitory. Rome no longer stood for continuity but for increasingly desperate crisis management. Alaric's successor Athaulf the Visigoth married into the imperial family. But the Visigoths were only part of a larger threat. From East to West the world seemed to be in convulsion. Vandals, Suevi, Franks and Huns as well as Ostrogoths and Visigoths were all on the move. Many reasons have been put forward for this unrelenting human tidal wave: increase of population, desiccation of pasture lands, a wish to move from nomadic lifestyle to more settled agriculture, or an ability to smell out weakness. Salvian, a hysterical priest from Marseilles, was sure it was divine retribution for Roman sexual misdemeanours. But the hordes were more terrifying than numerous. At most, all the invading horsemen and their families would have represented a tenth of the population of the Western empire. One to ten should have been eminently beatable odds, but for the fact that the invasion had been long nurtured from within.

Professor Browning says that we think today, in a world of nation-states with tight frontiers, that when there is an invasion there is a take-over and a complete replacement of administrative machinery. But this was not the case then. The Roman empire itself had been recruiting more and more 'barbarian soldiers' from across its frontiers for all sorts of reasons. Perhaps they were better fighting men; perhaps it was not so dangerous politically if they were killed. These soldiers were called Federates, and their recruitment was a process that had been going on since the end of the second century AD. The significant change that took place towards the end of the fourth century was that the Visigoths, who had been pushed by the Huns, asked permission to move over into Roman territory. They were received on the basis of being Federate soldiers – but then things went wrong.

The situation grew increasingly tense between the Roman officials and the leaders of the Visigoths. Finally the Federates turned their arms against their Roman masters. They threw them out and defeated the Roman army at the battle of Adrianople, where the emperor Valens was killed. In the end Valens' successor had to sign a treaty with the Visigoths, allowing them to settle in Roman territory as an independent state, with their own leaders and their own social and political structure. This marks a great change, not perhaps what we would think of as an invasion, but nevertheless it was very often the form of the barbarian invasions. The Visigoth leaders were often given military offices. They were appointed generals commanding the Roman army and slotted into society. For the Romans this was just a continuation of a practice of recruiting stalwart highlanders to fight their battles for them. For the Visigoths and others it meant they were part of the Roman empire, but were governed by their own laws and their own traditional mode of government.

Leo belonged to the Roman governing class which was now learning to compromise. A civil career would have been his for the asking, but he chose the church. Even as a young man he had a walk-on part in the great theological disputes of his day. Augustine mentions him as the young acolyte entrusted with carrying letters from Pope Zosimus to the bishops of Africa where the teachings of Jerome's old enemy the British heretic Pelagius were still causing problems. Leo climbed quickly up the hier-archical ladder. So little scandal was attached to his name that medieval hagiographers invented amorous peccadillos to give him something to

A rather docile-looking Alaric the Visigoth who shook Leo and Jerome's world by capturing Rome for three humiliating days

have triumphed over. Sometimes you will see Leo depicted with one hand or with a few fingers short. This is because later legends described how he had mutilated his hand after lusting after a married woman who had kissed his fingers. A good story, but who is the real Leo who speaks to us through his still preserved sermons and letters?

Dr Donald Allchin of St Saviour's Centre for Christian Spirituality, in Oxford, says we should think of a very solid character who can stand there in the gap when things are going wrong and can draw together his faith and his social and ethical action, because to him it is all one great indivisible scheme. God comes in Christ, Christ is present with us in the sacraments, and the sacraments bind us all together into a single body so that we are responsible for each other. That was Leo's understanding of his world and his faith. There was nothing at all privatised about his religion. He saw it as his Christian duty to be responsible for other people, and that comes over in his preaching. He had an extraordinary sense, which was shared by many of the early Christians, of human solidarity.

We are all members, he says, of one another. His sermons talk about how you have to care about the poor, to care about refugees, to care about the old. If you have slaves, you have to treat them as human beings. The master has to think of his slave as sharing the same human nature as himself. And because his whole theology was built round this idea that God actually becomes man, that God enters into our human situation fully, there is therefore something very precious about our humanity.

Leo was in an extraordinary situation. In the fifth century the Roman empire was collapsing, the barbarians were invading, everything was there for the taking. The Roman Church managed to take on something of the old power of the Roman empire because there was a power vacuum and Leo was a man with great ability as an administrator and as a ruler. But he was also a real bishop trying to preach the Gospel to his people.

Throughout the Mediterranean world, East and West, there was a conviction that all humanity was redeemable. Scores of lurid stories about reformed sinners passed from country to country like improving but titillating Chinese whispers. The heroes and heroines of these ecclesiastical penny dreadfuls would often come to be revered as saints. One of the most popular of these romances was the repentance of Pelagia. Sister Benedicta Ward SLG, Lecturer in History and Religion at the Centre for Medieval and Renaissance Studies, Oxford, says that according to the earliest account Pelagia was a very beautiful young woman who was famous for her jewellery. She was riding through the city one day, wearing practically nothing except the occasional pearl, when she and her young companions, who were laughing and singing, rode past a group of extremely serious-minded bishops. The bishops all hid their faces in a proper bishoply way, except for one Abbot Nonnus, who was from the desert. The accounts say that he gazed after her intensely as she rode away. The bishops looked slightly askance when they saw what was happening, but he said, 'Did you not see that great work of God go riding by? Was she not beautiful'?

The story then goes on that later Pelagia heard Nonnus preaching in a church and fell equally in love with him. She was baptised by him but immediately, being a very sensible woman, realised that this might go wrong, so she borrowed man's dress from him and ran away. The story concludes by describing how many years later James the deacon, who wrote the original account, went to Palestine. There Nonnus told him to go and visit a hermit called Pelagius. Pelagius was of course Pelagia, who had lived there as a hermit since she left her love for Nonnus and the world behind.

It was not only romances which made the journey from East to West. John Chrysostom, John Golden Mouth, the one-time archbishop of

Constantinople who referred to Pelagia's story in one of his sermons, was a teacher who influenced the whole church both East and West. He was an ascetic but first and foremost a preacher of unique power. He attacked those who abused wealth and high office. This was laudable but not a recipe for an easy life. Inevitably he acquired more highly-placed enemies, notably the wife of emperor Arcadius as well as his many admirers. His contribution to the Church, East and West, was immense. He concentrated on expounding the Bible in a way which appealed to non-scholars and was profound without being abstruse.

After Chrysostom's death, his associate John Cassian, an ascetic from Romania, was destined to shape the Western Church to an extent which is usually forgotten today. In 431, he was talent-spotted by Leo, who was not yet a priest but nevertheless already a theological troubleshooter. Leo saw that a potential storm was brewing at the Council of Ephesus where the ideas of the monk Nestorius were threatening the understanding of the nature of Jesus. Nestorius so separated the human and divine natures of Christ that he seemed to be advocating a schizophrenic saviour. Leo leant on the unwilling John Cassian, who had decided to give up writing, to produce a work on the nature of Christ on the eve of the Council. As a result of the Council, Nestorius was deposed by Cyril of Alexandria and John Cassian's book became the definitive word on Christ's nature. The partnership between Leo and Cassian was one of mutual admiration. Cassian describes Leo as 'the ornament of the Roman church and an honoured friend'.

Cassian fulfilled Leo's request, then withdrew from the theological boxing ring and went to southern France where, near modern Marseilles, he founded a monastery in the style of the Eastern desert monks – the sort of place where Pelagia's admirer, Nonnus, would have felt at home. There was some resentment from the local church at the effrontery of a foreigner bringing strange Egyptian monastic ideas where they were not particularly wanted. Professor Owen Chadwick, formerly Master of Selwyn College, Cambridge, and Chancellor of the University of East Anglia, says there were people who said that Cassian's undertaking was all nonsense. Whatever was this retreat from the world doing when people were needed to prop up the Roman empire, which was being attacked by barbarians? What were all these people achieving by merely saying their prayers and doing nothing about saving society? However, the movement somehow fits in, even in the West, with the ideals of the age. St Augustine at exactly that moment was writing a book called *The City of God,* in which he is moved by the sacking of the City of Rome, by Alaric the Visigoth, to compare the city of this world, which is perishable and will be destroyed, and the City of God which is absolutely imperishable and everlasting.

That was a very strong mood at that moment, so that, quite quickly, the critics were silenced and the monastic ideal began to take very quick root in the West.

After the Council of Ephesus, Leo's promotion to the throne of Peter was rapid. He became deacon and then archdeacon. He helped Cyril of Alexandria with a problem caused by Juvenal, the over-ambitious bishop of Jerusalem. When the easily forgettable pope Sixtus III died, Leo was out of Rome on a diplomatic mission trying to reconcile two squabbling military leaders, but there was no thought of an alternative papal contender. The people of Rome waited and when Leo returned he was unanimously elected pope and the papacy found itself in strong and determined hands. Dr Donald Allchin believes that this was a mixed blessing. Leo succeeded in making the papacy powerful, and many problems for Christendom arose because it was so powerful at that time when the Roman empire collapsed. This, he argues, is part of the complexity and the oddness of history – something which is good and necessary at that moment has consequences later which are not as good and quite unforeseen.

Leo obviously believed passionately that the see of Rome had been founded by St Peter and that he was St Peter's successor, so he certainly believed that he had a right and a duty to assume the responsibility of being the first bishop in the Christian world. But because there was such a power vacuum at that moment, all kinds of other things came to the papacy, beginning a very long process which goes on through the Middle Ages, in which it turns into a great temporal power as well as a spiritual power. And it was not only a matter of temporal power. Later popes would use the strong power base built by Leo as a battering ram of theological exclusivity. One of the victims would be Leo's friend John Cassian who was suspected of having been critical of St Augustine for being too passive in his belief about the relation between grace and man. Cassian believed man should not just wait on God but also had a responsibility to turn to God. This was seen as a veiled criticism of Augustine, and a blot on Cassian's reputation. Because of this, the Church was rather half-hearted about John Cassian and so gave him in effect a quarter feast day by placing it on 29 February.

Other Eastern influences on the Church fared better, in particular Mary the harlot, who lived and levitated in the time of Leo. She never set foot inside a church and yet to this day is venerated as a saint in the calendars of the East and the West. Sister Benedicta Ward explains why. Mary of Egypt lived in Alexandria, she left her parents when she was twelve, and the account says she looked around for what she was going to do and decided she was going to be a prostitute. She did not do it for money – she did spinning for money – but she just liked sex. One day she went down to the sea, and she saw some pilgrims going to Jerusalem on a boat. She had no money but she thought she could certainly pay her fare, and she did. She had seduced every man on the boat by the time it got to Jerusalem. There she pursued her usual way of life until the feast

Mary of Egypt, the harlot who lived and levitated in the time of Leo. She never set foot inside a church but is revered as a saint by Christians of the east and west

of the Holy Cross, when she tried to go with the pilgrims to venerate the Cross, and found she could not enter the Holy Sepulchre. She had a physical block and this suddenly made her think about what she had been doing and ask what kind of reality was left in her life.

She immediately turned her back on her former way of life and went over the Jordan into the desert, and lived there for about eighteen years absolutely alone, eating almost nothing. Just before she died, one of the desert monks, called Zosimus, met her and gave her the sacraments for the first time in her life. She was not a part of the clerical set-up or the hierarchy of the Church – and the contrast the story makes is between this good priest, who was nothing, and Mary, the converted harlot, who with nothing had everything. Zosimus went back the next year and found her lying dead on the sand. A lion came out of the desert to help him dig her grave. The lion seems to have found Zosimus rather a gossip, because while Zosimus was saying, 'Oh lion how absolutely dreadful this is, I don't know what we're going to do about burying her', the lion got busy with his paws, dug the grave, and then just walked off into the desert.

The popularity of Mary of Egypt was an admission that no matter how organised or hierarchical the churches were becoming there was always room for the irrationality of complete holiness. But on a more mundane level there was a need now, as never before, particularly in the Church of Rome for standing firm. As the confidence of the Western empire faded and Italy was crammed with refugees from the Vandal incursions in North Africa, Rome became aware of another threat – Attila, the son of Mundzuk. His sphere of influence stretched across Asia and Europe. It was believed he could call up winds and storms and no one could withstand his gaze. According to popular belief he was the inheritor of the iron sword of the Scythian war god.

So much for legend, but what are the facts? Professor Browning says that we have only one eye-witness account of him. It is by the Greek historian Priscus and we only have fragments. Priscus went in 449 on a mission to Attila's court, which was an enormous camp of wooden huts with a great dining hall in which Attila received his guests. Attila sat at a high table and it was observed of him that he ate from a wooden plate like the other Huns, and he was dressed exactly like them – the only difference was that his clothes were clean. Attila was the hereditary leader of a great confederation of nomadic people. These confederations held together while they were powerful but the moment they were defeated in battle they would break up and the separate groups would go off on their own and take their sheep and their cattle off to their own pastures. Attila's great empire was like that. It was tremendously powerful and mobile. His people of the Steppe did not merely ride one horse, they rode with a string of thirteen or fourteen. They jumped from one to another when each one was worn out and that is how they could cover 300 miles in a day. They had no industry, and even had to get weapons from the Romans by some means – so Attila had to keep pushing on, herding and trading captives for arms.

Attila was not the only one herding human cargo. While Leo had been climbing up the career ladder in Rome the other great church leader of the century had been struggling against very different odds. The young Roman Briton Patricius, the son of the deacon Calpurnius, had been captured by sea raiders at the age of sixteen and had been sold into slavery in Ireland. After a number of years he escaped and returned home. But in a dream he heard the voice of the people of Ireland coming across the bay of Foclut asking him to walk among them again. Patrick accepted the dream as an instruction to evangelise his former owners.

Patrick was a very different kind of person from Leo. As Dr Donald Allchin says, Leo was extremely self-assured. He knew he had the very best possible education and he belonged to the establishment. Poor old Patrick, as he says in his *Confession,* one of the most personal statements we have from that period, was uncertain of himself because he was painfully aware he had not had a good education. He knew his Latin was very poor – even when he is writing it he knows he is making grammatical and stylistic mistakes and he keeps apologising for them. He feels he has been pushed into the job of being a missionary and a preacher and a bishop almost against his will. He was a man who had been through an extreme experience of suffering and loneliness and must have been very near death as a teenager, and had some immense inner experience of God being with him. He spoke and taught out of that and after all God has a way of using people who are a bit broken. An immense legend has grown up about Patrick, but at the heart of it there is an anxious, almost frightened human being who is conscious that in himself he is not able to do God's work and yet he is doing it.

Patrick's faith was uncomplicated. Leo's world was fraught with more subtle difficulties. Eutyches the archimandrite insisted that the human nature of Christ was swamped by his divinity in the same way as a drop of wine would be lost in the sea. There had been a disastrous second synod at Ephesus, nicknamed by Leo the 'Robber Synod', where Eutyches had been acquitted – largely because he was in with the emperor Theodosius' court chamberlain, Chrysaphius. Leo's doctrinal paper had not even been read and Flavian, the patriarch of Constantinople, was fatally beaten up. Nothing had been solved. Theodosius died the following year and a new council was convened. Leo acted immediately and this time, as Dr Allchin says, to great effect. He sent a little document that he

*St Patrick, the former slave who returned to Ireland to bring the message of
Christianity to his erstwhile owners after hearing, in a dream, the voice of the
people of Ireland asking him to walk among them again*

had written earlier about the question of the two natures of Christ, and
the members of the Council concluded: 'Peter has spoken through Leo'.
It was a great moment. Somehow Leo had managed to state the belief and
the doctrine of the Church in such a way that it could actually be heard,
accepted and understood.

That little document, originally written for the Robber Synod, came
to be known as the *Tome of Leo*. It was the first major theological
contribution made by a pope and in the Roman Catholic church remains
the definitive statement on the nature of Christ fully man and fully God.
Leo was not only moulding orthodoxy but also the papacy. As Professor
Robert Markus, Emeritus Professor of Medieval History at Nottingham
University, says, Leo was certainly a milestone in devising a justification
for the authority of the bishop of Rome which is essentially based on the
Roman law of inheritance. He, the bishop of Rome, inherits the privilege
of Peter. But possibly more important is the fact that in the western
provinces and even in Italy the imperial administration was gradually
running down. The great symbol of this is that when Rome was under
attack, as it was twice during Leo's own pontificate, who was it who went
to intercede, in the first case with the Hun leader, Attila, and in the other
case with the Vandal king? It was the pope, the bishop of Rome, heading
an embassy of the local aristocracy. And this was symbolic of the kind of
symbiosis that had come into being between the Roman Church – its
bishop, its clergy – and the local aristocracy. The Church had taken over
the running of the city, its affairs, and this was happening at all sorts of
levels.

What Leo tried to establish was the kind of Christian urban community which was already beginning to take shape. Professor Markus is
sure that Leo had a conscious view of what he was trying to do. It may
not have been everybody's view. It is not our view of a society and in the
twentieth century it is very difficult to think of a municipal community
unified essentially on a religious basis, but that is what Leo was trying to
achieve. He set about it quite deliberately. We can see in his sermons and
in the liturgy that he is creating a new kind of urban community.

Leo's own prestige and the prestige of the papacy was greatly
increased by the parley with Attila. Leo, it seemed, had saved Rome from
invasion. In the later case of Gaiseric the Vandal king he is credited with
having saved it from the full horrors of pillage. But away from Rome the
power struggle between the empire and the barbarians was far from clear

cut. Professor Browning cites the example of a contemporary eye-witness account of what is going on from a little frontier town on the upper Danube in present-day Austria. It is from a life of the bishop – a man called St Severinus. A Germanic tribe was living in a settlement across the river from the town. There were some Roman soldiers on the Roman side in little garrisons in the town, and every year a man would come across the Alps with bags of gold and pay them. Occasionally other officials would come and try rather ineffectively to collect taxes. Gradually the pay does not come, and most of the soldiers just melt away and walk back home to Italy or settle on the land or set up home with a local girl.

In this little town where St Severinus lived, there was one soldier who did not depart and we can imagine him striding around this little town. He was not paid and we do not know how he lived, but he made it clear that he was a soldier and no doubt he wore a uniform and carried a sword. The Germans across the other side keep raiding for cattle or women, whatever they can get, and they also blackmail the town by threatening raids, so the citizens of this little town hire another group of Germans belonging to a different tribe to come and serve as their garrison because the Roman soldiers are no longer there to do it. Who is in control there?

Back in Rome, Leo had consolidated his position. There was no longer any doubt that the bishop of Rome was more important than the emperor. In the old days too the emperors used to take the title Pontifex Maximus – supreme priest – as a reminder that they had a say in religious matters. No more. The boot was now firmly on the other foot. As Dr Ian Woods, Senior Lecturer in Medieval History at the University of Leeds, explains, there was a shift from a period in which the structure of the Roman empire gave the Church a fairly clear position to a period when, with the Roman empire in the West having faded, the Church was having to establish itself in new ways. In that sense the papacy was certainly doing new things, both with regard to doctrinal issues, but also with regard to the buildings it was putting up in the City of Rome.

At the same time other quite interesting things were happening outside Rome, notably the very significant development in monasticism led by John Cassian, particularly around Lerin, just off the south coast of France, and in Marseilles. That was a very crucial development, because it sowed the seeds of the whole pattern which monasticism would take down to the eighth century.

So Leo's much-wronged friend John Cassian, the Romanian, would leave his mark on the Church of the West. But he achieved more – he popularised the seven deadly sins. As Professor Owen Chadwick explains, what we now call the seven deadly sins started off as eight. An Easterner called Evagrius was the first to list eight deadly sins and Cassian simply took them over. One of the eight sins is not one that we would immediately think of, that is accidie or boredom – particularly boredom with the monastic life. The first designers of the monastic ideal were very conscious of the difference between ideal and practice. You go into the desert to contemplate God and you take your Bible with you, and after a few days or a few weeks or a few months, you become dead bored. All sorts of precautions were taken to prevent this happening. But it was a sin to become dead bored – and a deadly one at that.

The West has made monasticism its own but it was an essentially Eastern idea. The stories of Mary the harlot and of Pelagia the penitent had such an international appeal, Sister Benedicta Ward believes, because they were a kind of poster, a vivid, crude reminder of what Christian faith is all fundamentally about. There was complete equality in the desert – it did not matter whether you were a man or a woman. Sister Benedicta wonders if being a harlot meant you had earned rather a lot of money and were therefore financially independent. You were not bound to obey a husband or a father, you had no obvious place in society, so to some extent you were free and could do what you liked. If you wanted to go off you could. You could burn your treasure. You could just cut out and go in a way that was less possible for a married woman or for the daughter of the house. Sister Benedicta would not, she says, like to think she is making any recommendations about prostitution as a preparation for monastic life, but perhaps there was a practical side to it then.

Leo died in 461 – about the time when Patrick died. The Roman empire of the West would last only another fifteen years. The last emperor, Romulus Augustulus, the namesake of the founder of Rome, was deposed by Odoacer the Herulian. Italy now had a barbarian king. In 493 he in turn was deposed by Theodoric the Ostrogoth.

But it was not a completely black picture, as Professor Browning explains. The great Ostrogothic king, Theodoric, who reigned for over thirty years in Italy, presided over what was, until his very last years, a very effective and friendly collaboration between the Goths, who bore arms and collected the rent, and the Romans, who collected what remained of the rents and maintained their administrative system. He was a *magister militum,* a commander in chief in the Roman army. Even as late as 508, when Clovis, a Frank, pushed across from the Meuse in Belgium and set himself up in Northern France, he clamoured for some sort of recognition and in that year he was actually appointed a consul by the emperor in Constantinople. It meant nothing in a sense, but it gave him authority and prestige in the eyes of his Roman subjects. The Germans, when they moved in, took over by and large the Roman administrative system of tax collecting, of law courts, and all the rest of the bureaucratic system. The Roman citizens continued to be governed by Roman law or what they could remember of it, while the Germans were governed by their own tribal laws.

The fifth century had a final theological sting in its tail. The tribes over the northern frontier of the Roman empire were converted to Arian Christianity, not to real Christianity, as the orthodox would call it, and in turn invaded and overthrew the Roman empire. So in place of the Roman empire the orthodox Christian empire was left with barbarian rulers who were, in fact, Christian heretics.

'Dearly beloved, the mercy of God the Father is beyond words. It softens the hearts of ferocious barbarians. Fallen natures can return to purity. Outsiders can become part of the family. Old sinful nature can be renewed in Christ who saves,' wrote Leo in his sermons which survived all the ravages which his city had to undergo. Dr Donald Allchin believes that that message of Leo's is still worth learning today. He thinks it is very important that we recognise that there are a great many things that we can learn from history and that when Christians study the history of the Church they are studying the history of their own family. They constantly find, in ages very different from their own, all kinds of extra-ordinary things which suddenly strike them as very familiar.

The fifth century, with the collapse of the empire and the destruction of a whole civilisation, was a period when people felt very insecure. In such a period people could find a deeper source of meaning, strength, and direction in life through their faith, and especially through this faith which Leo articulated and expressed so well – that God himself has entered into our human situation so we have a standing place in Jesus Christ which is independent of all the changes which can take place.

THE WORLD IN A SPECK
OF LIGHT

.

Nearly twenty years after two deaths – the death of Leo the Great, who had preached the Gospel and parleyed with Huns confident in the authority of Peter, and the death of Patrick the humble, who had been conscious of his weak spelling and had explained the Trinity by relying on a non-flowering weed – a child was born in northern Italy who more than any other single figure would shape the Western medieval world.

Unlike Leo, he was not born into the ruling class. Unlike Patrick, he had never experienced the degradation of slavery. He was no economist yet he dictated the economic framework of much of Europe for the next thousand years. He had little respect for the academic life and yet he would be venerated as the guardian of learning through the dark years to come. He is patron saint of Europe but he was no politician and never set foot outside Italy. Popes, cardinals, archbishops and bishops have looked to him as their spiritual father. He was not even a priest. His name was Benedict and in his middle age he had a vision which was described in detail by a pope called Gregory.

> *Servandus the deacon often used to visit Benedict the abbot. The two men would talk of God and the joys of heaven. One night when they had finished talking they retired each to his room. While the rest of the monastery slept Benedict stood praying at his window. Suddenly he saw a light pouring from the sky which was brighter than the sun at midday. And as he stared at the light he saw the whole world brought before him in a speck of light no larger than a sunbeam. Benedict shouted out to Servandus to come and witness the miracle. Servandus arrived in Benedict's cell while some of the midnight light remained.*

That vision, which Benedict was so anxious to share, lies at the heart of the success of the Benedictine way of life. By seeking God, men and women could acquire a uniquely sustaining sense of proportion. Compared to the love of God, the world of kings and conquerors was immeasurably small. The sunbeam vision was not a sign of megalomania. It was a recipe for sanity and survival.

Benedict's life straddles the fifth and sixth centuries – years rich in murder and madness. The Roman empire of the West had fallen. There were old power struggles and new overlords. Literacy was declining. A

St Benedict at prayer with cross and prayer book. Although Benedict was no great lover of the academic life he tried to strike a balance between work, prayer and study

Frankish king made hamfisted attempts at verse and tried to invent new letters for the alphabet. An Eastern emperor could not sign his name without a gold stencil. Later, in the East, a vaudeville actress turned empress would champion the old Monophysite heresy which proclaimed a Jesus whose humanity was swamped by his divinity.

The story of the sixth century is a tale of papal puns, religious riots, court murders, poetry and torture. Benedict had a hand in none of the great events of his day. His life story is one of practical sanctity and a dogged search for peace. His secret lay in the identity of his usually misidentified twin sister – but more of her later. Many legends have grown up round the historical Benedict. He could, it was believed, detect poison and make sunken iron float. He was a friend to ravens but a deadly enemy to nuns who talked in church. He could also hear men's silent thoughts. But apart from legend, can we be certain of any facts about his life?

Cardinal Basil Hume OSB, Archbishop of Westminster, Benedictine monk and former abbot, says Benedict was born in about the year 480 and as a young man went to Rome in order to study. His biographer, St Gregory, says that Benedict was scandalised by what he found in Rome among the students, and so he went off to a place called Subiaco, about twenty-five miles away, and lived there as a hermit. He was there for about three years and gradually people began to come and ask to be instructed by him and to have a way of life which is what we would now call a monastic way. It was almost accidentally that Benedict found himself instructing and teaching others how to live in community, how to praise God, and how to grow in the knowledge of the love of God.

Gregory says that Benedict wrote a *Rule* for monks that is remarkable for its discretion and its clarity of language. He goes on: anyone who wishes to know more about his character can discover in his *Rule* exactly what he was like as an abbot, for his life could not have differed from his teaching. That was a remarkable testimony because though Gregory was writing some forty or fifty years after Benedict's death, he did know disciples of Benedict and he had read Benedict's *Rule*.

That *Rule,* which holds the key to Benedict's life and character, is still followed today. It is unreservedly down-to-earth. You will never nowadays, it says, persuade all monks to give up wine, therefore insist only on moderation. And when it comes to food, make sure that the brother in charge of the provisions does not have too large an appetite. The abbot should look after those in his care like a wise physician, knowing that each has different requirements and abilities.

Benedict's *Rule* provided security and order in a world where certainty was in short supply. While Benedict was at Subiaco gathering his first monks into groups of twelve, the balance of political power in the outside world was more than usually precarious. Theodoric the Ostrogoth was king of Italy, nominally ruling on behalf of the Eastern emperor based in Constantinople. Theodoric was illiterate yet he found himself presiding over the last glimmers of classical Roman learning. Great scholars like Symmachus the Younger, Boethius the philosopher, and Cassiodorus the statesman were his subjects. And there was a further complication. Theodoric was an Arian heretic. His subjects were orthodox. It was a recipe for disaster and in 523 disaster struck when an unwanted instruction came from Constantinople.

The Reverend Michael Smith, church historian and Baptist minister of Golcar in West Yorkshire, sees it as the last spasm of classical learning. What happened was that the Eastern emperor, Justin, suddenly, out of the blue, decreed that all heretics should be barred from public office, which was a slap in the face for Theodoric. He immediately started looking round at all the noble Romans and he decided that all the orthodox Christians must be plotting against him. He became paranoid. He was by this time an old man and he went for one of the scholars – Symmachus. Boethius said, 'If you are attacking him, you must be attacking all of us.' Theodoric replied, 'Right, that's a confession of guilt – I'll have you as well,' and poor Boethius – a very cultured old man, as much Roman as a Christian – was slapped into gaol, tortured and eventually put to death.

It was while he was in gaol that he wrote the work for which he is famous, *On the Consolation of Philosophy*. This is a strange work, written by a man who was a Christian, but in the style of the best of pagan antiquity baptised into Christianity. It is a dialogue between Boethius and Lady Philosophy, talking about the ups and downs of life and how things are not always what they seem and how there is a hope of immortality – although strangely he does not base it at all on the resurrection of Jesus. It was the last little sand-castle of Roman antiquity before the barbarian tide flowed over it. When Boethius was executed and his friend Cassiodorus retired to his monastery down in the south of Italy, that was the final snuffing out of classical antiquity.

Benedict too had his problems. Various attempts were made to remove or at least to discredit him. In one case an entire troglodyte monastery who had invited him to take over as abbot decided that his ideas of reform were beyond a joke. He would have to go. A monastic conspiracy was hatched. The monks poisoned the wine to be served in the refectory. But when Benedict blessed the wine the flagon containing the malevolent wine shattered. Benedict immediately realised what had happened. He took it as a signal not for punishment but for the next move.

As David Wright, Senior Lecturer in Ecclesiastical History at New College, Edinburgh, explains, Benedict decided that the monks were irreformable and said that there was no point in his trying to lead them in the life that was the quest for God. So he took himself off to Monte Cassino, the prominent hill-site midway between Rome and Naples. There, round about 529, he started to build his own community, and it was for that community that he wrote the famous *Rule*, the *Regula Monachorum*, that has had such an enormous influence in Western monasticism in the subsequent centuries.

It is important to remember that Benedict's *Rule* was neither the first rule nor the only rule. Pachomius of Egypt, Basil of Caesarea and Cassian of Marseilles had all written on the monastic life. There was also the anonymous *Rule of the Master* which contained valuable advice on how to blow your nose in a manner least likely to upset the angels. So what did Benedict's rule have that the others did not? The Reverend Michael Smith believes that it had three strengths. First, Benedict insisted on people sticking to their particular commune and not wandering around. There were lots of people who, as soon as they got fed up with one monastery, pushed off to another. John Cassian has a lovely description of the attitude of mind of people like that, and you get them today, shunting around from one church to another, looking for the perfect church, and of course they never find it.

The second strength was that he had a good balance between manual labour, worship and study and this was very important. There was none of the wild asceticism of the East, or of the Celts, where you could get six lashes for failing to say Amen after grace.

The third strength was the idea of the work of a monk being to copy manuscripts. As a consequence the whole wisdom of classical antiquity was preserved.

But the Benedictine *Rule* is, and was emphatically, not simply for intellectuals. In his youth, Benedict had not been impressed by the academic way of life. When he was in Rome he had abandoned his studies, and since he was there with a nurse rather than with a tutor, it is most likely that he dropped out at what we would think of as sixth-form level. In a famous phrase Gregory hints that Benedict saw through the shallowness of scholarship for its own sake. He left Rome, he says, 'wisely unlearned'.

Benedict's *Rule* is not a theological treatise, but rather a monastic handbook. It deals with such issues as how to get into the monastery, the sleeping arrangements for the monks, and matters of food. Central to it is the pattern of worship in the chapel of the monastery, seven times a day – the monastic hours as they come to be called later. Benedict calls them the Opus Dei, the work of God. The work of God, he says, is prayer and worship, and that is right at the heart of the monastic life that Benedict provides for in this *Rule*. But the *Rule* covers many other things including the dangers that arise when monks travel abroad. It is essential to Benedict's monastery that everything necessary for daily life is contained within it. Sometimes the monks would need to move outside the walls for agricultural work, but the ideal is that the monks stay within the confines of the monastic walls because wandering abroad, as Benedict says, is not good for their souls.

Benedict's idea of an ideal community has been pursued in every single century since his own. But Benedict was not born out of time. As Dom Henry Wansbrough OSB, monk of Ampleforth Abbey, Yorkshire, says, Benedict fitted into his world in a most remarkable way. It was a world where the barbarian darkness was beginning. The standard of civilisation had dropped and Benedict was writing for a fairly primitive society. He insists that during Lent monks should read a book, but he does not envisage that there would be anything like the amount of reading and writing and study that there would have been 150 years before. His society is primarily an agricultural one.

The *Rule* would prove itself adaptable to all conditions of life. Benedictine monasteries flourish in countries Benedict never heard of. And it is a *Rule* for women as well as for men. Dame Felicitas Corrigan

OSB, a Benedictine nun of Stanbrook Abbey in Worcestershire, pointed out that the people who really adopted the Benedictine Rule for nuns, as well as monks, were the English. St Augustine brought knowledge of the *Rule* of St Benedict when he came to Canterbury in 597 and it spread like wildfire all over England, so that England became the first wholly Benedictine country. England took to the *Rule* like Benedictine ducks to water.

Dame Felicitas believes that Benedict's *Rule* has moulded the character of the English – partly because they are like the Romans in temperament – they like law and order, they are very practical and pragmatic, and they do not go in for rarefied mysticism. The *Rule* suited the English temperament and also the English fondness for ceremonial – Benedict has left his stamp on England in many ways – what are traditional university gowns but adapted Benedictine cowls and habits?

Benedict had not been the only one laying down the law. While he was sitting in the monastic eyrie of Monte Cassino putting the final touches on the rule of life for generations of monks and nuns to come, across the Christian world in Constantinople a very different operation was in full swing. Justinian, the emperor, who had great difficulty in sitting still, was codifying Roman law from all the centuries past. He seems to quote from Benedict's *Rule* on at least three occasions. He was a reserved, cerebral man responsible for the building of Hagia Sophia, acclaimed as the most beautiful church in the whole of Christendom, but he and his empress Theodora had their enemies. Justinian was a strange character. His official biographer, Procopius, says that he considers that Justinian was nothing less than a demon in a human body. The Reverend Michael Smith says he has rather more sympathy with Theodora than he has with Justinian. Justinian was a very inward-turned man. When you look at some of the mosaic portraits of him you can see a weak man, whereas Theodora, whatever her faults, was strong and consistent. Justinian was rigidly orthodox. Theodora was an ex-prostitute from Alexandria who had been converted by Monophysite monks and so she was ardently Monophysite herself. She was quite ready, when Justinian was turning against the Monophysites, to hide the Monophysite monks in her part of the palace.

When the football hooligans of the day, the chariot race supporters, turned against Justinian, burned down Constantinople and had him besieged in the palace, he did not know what to do. He was all for abdicating. Theodora turned and said, in effect, 'Get up you wretched wimp – you might as well stand up and fight: for my part, I believe the imperial purple is the best shroud of all.' And she set General Belisarius on the mob and sent out somebody to bribe some of them to break ranks. She was a great power behind the throne. They called her 'Despoina', the lady, the mistress – a title she fully deserved.

The formidable Theodora, the former prostitute turned empress, surrounded by courtiers. She was equally at home sheltering Monophysite monks or quieting the sixth-century equivalents of football hooligans

Pope Gregory the Great was the former papal legate at Constantinople and was traditionally credited as the biographer of Benedict. On the face of it the two men have little in common. But for Gregory, Benedict the powerless represented the ideal Christian way of life. Father Francis Walker SJ, Head of the Department of Ecclesiastical History at Heythrop College, London, believes that Gregory was a monk manqué.

As a young man Gregory had become a monk. He had left his public office as prefect of Rome and sold all his possessions. His family had vast estates in Sicily and from these and the money that was accruing to him he founded several monasteries and himself joined his own monastery in Rome on the Caelian Hill, as a simple monk. He was accustomed to ruling and governing the city as part of the administration; he rejected it all in order to seek the life of contemplation and prayer. Nonetheless when he was forced to become pope, he again took up the administrative role of the chief diocese in Italy in very difficult circumstances.

Gregory became very much an active, ruling pope with a great concern for the welfare of the people in Rome, and in Italy generally, in terms of their welfare as citizens. He had protected them dramatically from the Lombards who invaded Northern Italy and besieged Rome. But the monastic way was terribly important to him, because it was his ideal of life, namely the union with God – the search for perfect peace and that mystical union which he believed he could find in the monastic way of life. Even as pope in his later years, he said it was that interior calm which should be recognised as the most valuable thing in his life. Frequently he said that he regretted having turned away from it. Gregory is a fascinating example of somebody pulled two ways – somebody who saw that you could be attracted to the transcendental in religion, but in order to pursue it, you cannot refuse to do the other tasks that are presented to you. If other people need the Gospel message and need help, then it is a false sort of perfection to turn away from their need. He had very strong views on this, that one can be in love with silence, contemplation, prayer and union with the Almighty, but one can never make that a goal which is so overwhelming that one abandons the duties of a Christian. He was very much a man of the Roman world in the sense that his idea of duty and service to others was paramount. He was not a democrat in any sense. He belonged to the old senatorial rank of the late Roman empire, and his idea was that one had a duty to fulfil, in some station in life, and he found that in the office of the bishop of Rome.

For Gregory the monk manqué, as for many others, one of the most attractive features of Benedict's *Rule* was its insistence on stability. Once you joined a community you stayed there. It became your family and your home. On the western edge of Christendom, monasticism was wilder. Irish monks, like the great Columba of Iona, were not in the Benedictine mould, as the Reverend Michael Smith explains. To be an Irish monk, he says, you had to be a combination of an SAS man and a Himalayan mountain goat, because the Irish, and the Celtic Church generally, were old-fashioned and severe. It had some rigorous penitential piety which was not quite in line with the more easy-going Benedictines. It was hard asceticism which had been hammered out in the deserts of Egypt and Syria and then translated to the North Atlantic winter's wind, sleet and snow. So you can imagine that anybody who was involved in Irish monasticism was a pretty hard man to start with. From what we can gather, part of the reason why Columba went on his travels was because of some terrible quarrel in which blood was spilt. Certainly he was up before a Church Synod, excommunicated and then reinstated. The upshot of it was that he found Ulster too hot for him and decided he would move to the little island which is now called Iona.

From Rome Gregory was looking westwards. He believed that the barbarians who flooded over the Western empire should have the Christian message preached to them. They should be converted, they should be saved, as he put it, by being gathered into the band of the chosen. And he saw life very much in those terms. In the midst of wars, famines and plagues, he wanted to gather as many as possible into the kingdom of Christ. So when he met, as the story goes, the Angle slave boys in Rome who had been brought from what would be the very farthest outreach of the Roman empire, he was concerned that there was a group of human beings who had not had the Gospel preached to them. So he vowed to send his missionaries. In fact, the story goes that he wanted to go himself but was bishop of Rome and was not free to do that. The story has a charm about it – it has been much disputed by historians since, but there is no reason not to think that, in spite of embroidery, it was a real event and that he was aware of these people from Britain.

While Gregory was considering the mission to the English, disaster fell on Benedict's monastery at Monte Cassino. As he had prophesied, it was destroyed by the Lombards, the last of the invading Germanic tribes still infected by the old Arian heresy. The monastery was in ruins and this ensured Benedict's success. The fugitive monks went to Rome, the most central point for propagating new religious ideas. Benedict's ideal of life was now literally at the heart of the Western church.

Did this give Benedict an unfair prominence? Does he deserve to be called the Father of Western monasticism? Dom Henry Wansbrough does not think that something as great and important as Western monasticism can be the child of one person. But it seems to him that the great contribution of the *Regula Monachorum* – the *Rule* – is its practicality, particularly when compared with other contemporary monastic rules.

In Rome at the end of the sixth century, during pope Gregory's reign, there was a consciousness of the need for a new framework of religious and political power. Father Walker thinks a large element in Gregory's world view was that he thought it was coming to an end, and very soon. He foresaw the decline of the Roman empire and saw his own position in Rome as being the shepherd of a flock at the end of time. That was why he was so insistent on gathering the Anglo-Saxons and the Germanic tribes. They had to be brought in before the end of time comes, before the great judgement.

But in fact Gregory stands at the beginning of a huge new development because, finding that Constantinople of the Eastern empire was going to be no use to him as a support to keep things going, he then turned to the Franks, to the Lombards themselves, and to the Visigoths, to build up a new Church in the West in which he, the pope, will be the only person of significance. He is the founder pope of the Church of the Middle Ages in the West and it is there that his great fame rests. The papacy would dominate the religious life of the Middle Ages.

St Columba, the first known witness of the Loch Ness monster, setting off for Iona to convert souls in recompense for those killed at the battle of Cooldrevne,

From now on, because of Benedict's *Rule,* monasticism would be thought of as primarily an exercise in *community* living, not merely as the pursuit of solitary holiness. Professor Robert Markus says it was a high point in a development towards a much more socially-conceived form of monasticism. What was new was that monasticism began to be considered not so much as self-denial, the renunciation of marriage, of worldly goods and status and all the rest of it, but as the life of the perfect community, the life of dedication to the brethren, or the sisters, the life of charity. Every duty in the community becomes a work of love. The government of the abbot is like that of a family. It becomes a unique kind of society.

They are still celibate of course, they are still property-less, but the
emphasis is on the common life. Benedict legislated for a monastery very
much on those lines. In the Greek world, St Basil was moving in the same
direction – with the emphasis not so much on asceticism and renunciation,
but on the life of the community.

   Throughout the last half of his life, Benedict was content to rule his
monks. He was not interested in the larger world stage, but secular rulers
were interested in him. He was visited by Totila, the king of the Goths,
who arrived determined to outwit the holy man and left in awe of his
wisdom. Benedict was regarded as an innovator and a practical genius by
his contemporaries. And David Wright believes he does deserve to be
called a genius. He provides in his *Rule* one of the things that later leads
to the unification of Europe. It is appropriate to call him a founder of

Europe – or one of the fathers of Europe – because he sets out one of the great unifying features of the medieval European world. One has to see him as a person of profound gifts, insight and balance. It is interesting that one of the qualities that Gregory ascribes to the *Rule* is the word discretion – which means soundness of judgement. Benedict has a very sure touch for the pressure points of people living together in communities, and it is this balance in the *Rule* between a pretty firm discipline (ultimately the abbot could be an autocrat – and that was one of the problems of later monasteries) and authority, together with consideration for the weak and a really fine insight into what makes people tick when they live together.

St Benedict in his old age receiving Totila, king of the Goths. Totila, who seems to have had a rather feeble sense of humour, swapped clothes with one of his courtiers. Benedict saw through the disguise immediately

According to some traditions Benedict had a twin sister called Scholastica to whom he was devoted, and whom he visited just before he died. Dom Henry Wansbrough believes she is the hidden strength behind the Benedictine ideal. The story of Scholastica is one brief chapter in the second book of St Gregory's dialogues and she is described as the sister of Benedict. She was a woman of prayer too, and Benedict and his sister used to meet once a year for a day. Gregory introduces the story as a story of the power of prayer because on the last time they met Scholastica wanted Benedict to stay instead of going back to the monastery for vespers in the evening. Benedict refused – being a true monk he knew that he had to return to his community for vespers. Scholastica then prayed that he should be forced to stay and as a result of her prayer such a thunderstorm broke out that Benedict had no choice. This is more than a pretty tale of sisterly affection – Scholastica the twin is a typical figure. Scholastica means the woman of contemplation, just as Benedict means the blessed man, for Benedict is Gregory's ideal of the blessed man, living the blessed life, which he himself could not lead as the pope and administrator. Scholastica similarly is the figure of contemplation, a feminine figure, rather like the figure of Wisdom in the Bible. Gregory is trying to say that every year, for a certain time, Benedict went off to pray on his own with his sister Scholastica who was a symbol of contemplation, rather as St Francis talks about Brother Light and Brother Sun and Sister Moon. Towards the end of his life, Benedict was delayed in contemplation. He did not return to the ordinary duties, but stayed in an extended period of prayer. As he himself says in the *Rule*, prayer should be short and pure unless it is extended under the inspiration of the Holy Spirit.

To future generations, Benedict and his *Rule* would offer an ideal of life based on an unchanging bedrock of contemplation, yet flexible enough to adapt to, and to help form, a changing world. Cardinal Hume says that in Benedictine monasteries a chapter of the *Rule* of St Benedict is read every day so that the principles of the *Rule* are put in front of modern Benedictines day by day. However in every monastery there are also the constitutions which are the adaptation to contemporary society and the needs of every particular monastery. The Benedictine world is not a centralised world – every monastery is autonomous, independent of another. The monasteries are loosely bound in a congregation, and the congregations are loosely bound into a confederation.

The principles of the *Rule* are adapted to the needs of the age. There is always a problem when you adapt an ancient document to contemporary needs because you have to be very careful not to compromise what is important. However, some of the *Rule* is quaint to modern ears, Cardinal Hume admits. For instance, St Benedict does not want his monks to sleep with their knives round their waists, which is obviously not a temptation to which modern monks succumb. It also encourages, or rather allows, corporal punishment if monks are obtuse. Benedict was, after all, dealing with some pretty tough Goths. The *Rule* has survived because it is moderate, sensible, and takes into account the foibles and the weaknesses of human nature. The strong always have something to strive after and the weak should not feel oppressed and depressed. Cardinal Hume thinks that all people who occupy positions of leadership, whether in the world of the Church or even in the secular world, would do well to read the two chapters on the abbot. It is, he says, very wise advice on how to handle other people which carries across the centuries with all the unruffled certainty of a man who knew that compared to the Kingdom of God, all that is in this world can be contained in a speck of light.

A NECKLACE FROM
NORTHUMBRIA
·

In the early years of the seventh century, somewhere between the death of Gregory the Great, the biographer of Benedict and papal punner, whose observation that some fair-haired slave boys were not angles but angels had launched a mission to the English, somewhere between his death and the birth of Mohammed, the honest one, the prophet of Allah whose message would strike fear into the heart of Christendom, a Northumbrian princess called Breguswitha had a dream about a piece of jewellery.

> *While Breguswitha's husband was in exile in the court of the British king Cerdic and while their daughter was very small, Breguswitha had a strange prophetic dream. She dreamt that her husband had been taken away and try as she might she could not find him anywhere. Then while she was anxiously searching for him she suddenly came across a most valuable necklace hidden under her clothes. It seemed to shine with such brilliance that all Britain was filled with the splendour of its light.*

That dream, we are told, was amply fulfilled by the life of Breguswitha's daughter Hild, more widely known today as Hilda of Whitby, the ecclesiastical diplomat and bishop-maker, the first patron of English poetry, whose goodness, according to Bede the historian, was so obvious that it softened the hearts not only of those who knew her but also of those who only heard about her.

Hilda's life spanned most of the seventh century. It was a century of clashes and conformity – a time when old dynasties were crumbling and new power bases were in the making. With the aid of hindsight the first flicker of a fallen Constantinople can be seen in the siege by the Persians and Avars. The Holy Roman empire is a twinkle in the eye of the mayors of the palace who take control from the increasingly weak and mad Frankish royal family. Arab successes in Palestine, North Africa and Egypt are the first coals laid on that furnace of fear, resentment, faith and greed which will become the crusades. But these are problems for the future. In the church of the East, the old controversies about the nature of Christ rumbled on and on the far edges of the Western Church there was a flowering of learning and faith which put the rest of Europe in the shade.

This was Hilda's world – a world where Christianity was com-

St Hilda of Whitby, the formidable princess, abbess and bishop-maker

paratively young and was expressed with a delight and an exuberance which we can see today at first hand in the extravagantly intricate beauty of the Lindisfarne Gospels. And Hilda of Whitby, Sister Benedicta Ward believes, is the ideal ambassador for that age. Hilda, she says, is someone who touches every aspect of life in that marvellous century in England, that seventh century when for the first time it is possible to see the *gens Anglorum*, the English people, emerging. Hilda was born about 614, the daughter of Hereric and Breguswitha. She was baptised with her great uncle, Edwin, by Paulinus at York and lived at the court of Edwin for quite a time. Bede says that for thirty-three years she lived as a secular princess, unmarried. At thirty-three she went to East Anglia, where her sister had been the queen, intending to become a nun. She wanted to go to Chelles, near Paris, but Aidan, the Irish converter of Northumbria, asked her to come back and be a nun in Northumbria. So she returned and became a nun, first on a piece of land near the River Weir, then at Hartlepool, and finally at Whitby.

The monastery at Whitby was a double foundation comprising a community of nuns and a community of monks. It is an unexplained phenomenon of seventh-century Western Europe that such establishments flourished. They were always headed by an abbess rather than an abbot. Hilda's position involved more than ecclesiastical administration. She was responsible for the lay brothers who worked the monastery's farmland and furthermore clearly had some sort of pastoral brief for the area surrounding the monastery. Bede tells us that her advice was sought both by ordinary people and by local rulers. She also tried to raise the standards of learning and behaviour among those who would be considered for training as priests. In this, she must have been fairly successful. Bede records that no fewer than five of Hilda's protégés eventually became bishops, including the unlovable and pompous Wilfred.

But Gerald Bonner, Reader in Theology at the University of Durham, believes that it was not Hilda's administrative efficiency which earned her such an eminent place in Bede's *History of the English Church and People*. Bede admired her, he says, because he saw in her evidence of sanctity. He particularly mentions that she was always concerned in exhorting her monks and her nuns, first and foremost, to keep peace with one another and to love one another. This seems to have been the pattern of her life. Bede mentions that she was commonly referred to by everybody as Mother, and this does not appear to have been, in her case, a technical religious term for an abbess. It seems to have come from genuine love and regard for her.

Hilda was Northumbrian. She had been baptised by a Roman missionary but her style was Celtic. At Whitby she seems to have drawn on the unyielding rule of Columbanus the quarrelsome, an outspoken Irish monk who enjoyed writing insulting letters to popes, upsetting royalty and jumping to conclusions. He was a great traveller and took his own style of punitive monasticism as far south as Bobbio in Italy, where to this day you can see traces of Irish-style handwriting in the earliest monastic documents.

Hilda managed to reconcile different types of churchmanship. Others found this more difficult. Much harm was done, Bede tells us, at the very beginning of the seventh century when there was a meeting between Augustine of Canterbury and some of the British bishops who followed the Celtic customs in matters of discipline, liturgy, haircuts and the dating of Easter. Before the meeting the bishops consulted a hermit who told them they would be able to judge Augustine's worth as a man of God by his actions. If he stood to greet them, he was a humble servant of Christ and should be revered. If he remained seated, he was arrogant and should be despised. Augustine who was in the last year of his life remained seated. There was no meeting of minds.

The differences between Celtic and Roman practices undoubtedly caused tension. But tension is not schism. Later historians have painted a picture of a unified, plucky Celtic Church bravely playing David to the Goliath of Rome. Patrick Wormald, Lecturer in Medieval History at the University of Glasgow and a British Academy Researcher in Humanities, believes it is time for that myth to be debunked once and for all. He says that the Celtic church is undoubtedly an invention by subsequent historians. Every local church had its own particular traditions and its own liturgies. The line taken, for example, by pope Gregory the Great was that it was wonderful that there were so many different traditions in the church. So there was nothing exceptional about Irishmen or Welshmen having their own ways of doing things in the seventh century.

Indeed the idea of a unified Celtic Church does not stand up from a Celtic point of view. There was very little in common between the Irish and the Welsh churches of that date. The one thing they shared, which may have produced the whole illusion in the first place, was a particular way of calculating the day of Easter. This was described in great detail by Bede, the most powerful and eloquent historian of the millennium, so that it came to seem an even greater and more decisive issue than it was. The fact that the Welsh and the Irish did agree on that one thing has caused them to be lumped together and seen as the same. But neither the Welsh nor the Irish knew that they spoke the same Celtic language. Their languages were so distinct they were not aware of their common origins.

The Irish knew that they owed their Christianity in the first place to Roman Britons like Patrick, but they had developed their own distinctively Irish ways of doing things. It is legitimate to talk about Irish Christianity as something quite important and identifiable, so long as one does not then go on to think that there was any spirit of rebelliousness or desire for division. On the contrary the Irish, as perhaps you might expect, were to the forefront in boosting the cult of St Peter and the acknowledgement of papal authority in seventh-century Europe.

It is equally misguided, Dr Jinty Nelson, Lecturer in History at King's College, London, believes, to see the evangelisation of England as a two-horse race between Roman and Irish missionaries. It is a false picture in the sense that Christianity came to the Anglo-Saxons from many sides,

St Augustine, the first archbishop of Canterbury. He was an efficient missionary sent to England by pope Gregory the Great. He managed to ruffle indigenous episcopal feathers

not just Rome or Iona but directly from Gaul as well. All these influences, all these missions, were coming to bear in the Anglo-Saxons simultaneously. It was a mix, and Hilda's career embodies that. She planned to go to Gaul and she did not see her plans as contradictory to the messages she was getting from Iona via Aidan. Nor did she see the Roman connection as hostile to her other brands of Christianity. They were all one brand for her.

Bede is the first prose author of Anglo-Saxon blood whose name is known to us. His life just overlapped with Hilda's, and he was the only Englishman identified by Dante in Paradise. Another tradition claims that an angel wrote the epitaph on his tomb. It is largely through his eyes that we can see the development of the seventh-century English church. But

A tonsured scribe at work, most probably Bede, the first English prose writer and the only Englishman identified by Dante in Paradise

what manner of man was he? Gerald Bonner says that the first thing to remember about Bede is that he was a natural writer and historian, but his motives for writing are essentially pastoral. He is concerned, first and foremost, to make available knowledge of the scriptures and knowledge of earlier Christian writers to people less able than himself or less willing to work than himself. In his famous commentary on the Apocalypse, he says that he is writing it because he finds that there is a laziness about the English people which makes them reluctant to read long books. Bede should be seen primarily as the scholarly pastor, who wants to teach the faith. In addition, he writes on matters of considerable concern in Northumbria in the seventh and eighth centuries, such as how to calculate the date of Easter. When he comes to write *The History of the English Church and People* at the end of his life, his concern is to carry on the story of the message of the Gospel given in the New Testament. He wants to show how Christ's Church has grown and flourished and finally extended itself to Britain, a country which had been cut off from Christianity precisely because of the invasion and settlement of Bede's own people. Bede is a very unegoistical writer and does not indulge in talking about himself, but the more one reads him, the more one gets a feeling of friendliness and intimacy about him. He is one of the people with whom one could happily spend a day in conversation – which is not always true of some of the earlier saints.

Bede was a prolific writer, but first he was a monk. No matter how many projects he had on hand he would always attend the chanting of the Psalms which made up the monastic day. Otherwise, he said, the angels would be asking one another, 'Where is Bede?' Bede was a historian and an honest historian but his history was written with a purpose. Dr Nelson says that Bede was trying to do something with his *History* in the 730s that is not what modern historians are trying to do when they write history books. He was trying to present a story which emphasises the special nature of the English as a united nation. The pope sends the mission to the English and what is then created is a Church of the English. In the seventh century there was no such thing as the English *gens* – the English people were only emerging. In a sense Bede constructed that people on the model of the holy people in the Bible, the people of Israel. Other continental barbarian people said exactly the same thing. The Franks called themselves the New Israel and so did the Visigoths in Spain. So it is not surprising that Bede tried to do the same, but it is important to realise that he is using an Old Testament model to understand his own world.

Bede was not the only one using the Old Testament model. The Irish monks working in Scotland and Northern England were holy men very much in the mould of the Old Testament prophets, but there is another element which is often overlooked. The Irish monks also drew on the traditions of the *filid* or druid class. These outspoken learned holy men, who travelled round working wonders, prophesying the future, retelling the past and having no fear of present anger, whether of kings or of natural calamities, had long been the linchpin of pagan Irish society. Dr Wormald believes that the memory of that druid class partly explains why the Irish achieved more lasting results than the missionaries sent from Rome. There was a pagan reaction in Kent, and in pretty well every kingdom converted in seventh-century England by continental or Italian missionaries, but not a single one of those relapses in areas converted by Irish missionaries. His explanation for that is that Irishmen, being essentially barbarian nobles themselves, understood very well the importance of the ancestor and the values of the past to any warrior nobility. So they were prepared to tell their converts at courts that they did not have to worry about their great ancestors – that God would have saved them as he had saved all the great heroes of the Irish past. It is an interesting irony that although the Irish were much tougher on pagan cults and did not believe in converting temples, they were certainly more tolerant towards the pagan past. This may explain why conversion from the Irish was more lasting to a warrior nobility than conversion from Rome.

The two styles of Christian practice existed uneasily side by side. In 664 moves towards reconciliation were finally made. King Oswy of Northumbria followed the Roman customs for dating Easter. His wife followed the Celtic way. Oswy summoned all parties to meet for a synod to be held at Hilda's abbey at Whitby. Colman spoke for the Irish side, Wilfred for the Roman. In calling the synod, Oswy's motives were not only theological: there was a domestic crisis to resolve as well. Sister Benedicta Ward sees it as a problem at the breakfast table: that Oswy and his queen had boiled eggs at different times during Lent. It was not just the date of Easter that was problematic, it was the period of the fast beforehand. If, in the royal household, the king started fasting two weeks or three weeks before the queen, or vice versa, there might have been problems on a domestic level. To us it looks a trivial point, but it was not at the time. Easter was the centre of the Christian year and everything else came to and from it.

At the Council of Whitby there were extremely complicated arguments about arithmetic, such as how the year should be calculated, for hour after hour. In the end, the king asked Colman, 'Right, on whose authority do you, Colman, speak?' 'Columba's.'

'On whose authority do you Wilfred speak?' 'St Peter's.'

'Well,' said Oswy, 'I know that when I die St Peter is the keeper of the keys of the kingdom of heaven and I certainly want to get through into heaven, so I vote for Peter and the Roman calculation.' He did not actually decide on the evidence, but upon authority.

Authority was the key word in the Whitby debate. More was at stake than the calendar. Professor John MacQueen, Professor of Scottish Literature and Oral Tradition at the University of Edinburgh, says that there were also discussions about the position of bishops in the Church. Theologically the Celtic bishops had all the authority that bishops had in the Roman Church, in terms of divine service and consecration of priests. What they lacked was any kind of diocesan authority. Dioceses did not exist, largely because the Celtic lands had been outside the territory of the Roman empire and dioceses derived from the old imperial bureaucratic structure. The people who had most power were the abbots, because the Church tended to be organised into monasteries. The abbot of a mother house had authority over his daughter houses as well as his mother house. He might very well have a bishop or several bishops living in these houses. The abbot would allow the bishop authority as far as the distinctively bishop's authority would go, but where administrative authority was concerned, he kept it to himself.

Dr Nelson says that Hilda, abbess of Whitby, was on the side of the Celts. But she thinks that the whole significance of this conflict between Roman and Celtic has been overstressed. The peculiarities of the Celtic Church have been exaggerated and misrepresented. It was not cut off: it had many contacts with Spain, with Frankia, even with Rome and with the East Mediterranean world, so that the kind of Christianity that was being practised and preached by Aidan who came from Iona was not as different, as Bede perhaps pretends, from the Christianity that was coming from Rome.

At the end of the synod, Bede tells us, all those who had supported the Irish date for Easter renounced it. It was a victory for bishop Wilfred, a former pupil of Hilda's. From then on all Western Christendom would celebrate Easter on the same day. But how had the divergence come about in the first place? Professor MacQueen says that essentially the problem lay in the fact that Easter was calculated in terms of the moon, but also in terms of the sun. It went back to the Jewish calendar and the way the Feast of the Passover used to be fixed. The crucifixion was related to the Feast of the Passover. So the way of fixing Good Friday and Easter Day was by way of the first full moon that followed the vernal equinox on 21 March. That could move over a very considerable period and there were various ways of calculating it. The Celts used something which had been standard throughout the Christian world some centuries before, which was a solar cycle of eighty years. Since then there had been introduced a new solar cycle which only occupied eighteen years, and the two did not

always coincide. So Whitby corrected that Irish calendar time warp. The church in Britain evangelised from the West by the Irish monks and from the East by a mixture of Greek, North African, Italian and Frankish missionaries was anything but insular.

The final chapters of Bede's *History* record the advent in Europe of a most terrible human plague, the curse of the Saracens. The Arabs, first- and second-generation Muslims, who had taken Palestine, North Africa and Egypt, were the followers of the greatest religious figure of the seventh century, Mohammed the visionary of Mecca. He described how he had visited heaven on a magic donkey mule and preached a message of Islam, or surrender to the one God – a message which Professor Anthony Bryer, Director of the Centre for Byzantine, Ottoman and Modern Greek Studies at Birmingham University, says should not be seen in isolation from Christianity, and in particular from the beliefs of those Eastern Christians who still clung to the Monophysite heresy which had difficulty in accepting Christ as fully human as well as divine. In ordinary history books, he says, you turn the page and you suddenly find a chapter headed 'Islam'. You have not been told anything about Islam before, and the Muslims seem to come straight out of the desert. But Islam did not spring fully-armed into the world. It belongs to one of the emerging peoples of the East, who include the Monophysites. St John of Damascus regarded Islam as the hundred and first heresy. To Eastern Christian ears it sounded familiar – an extreme form of the Monophysite creed, with its emphasis on the oneness of God and its rejection of Greek tinkering with the Trinity.

The message which Mohammed preached was rooted in belief in the God of Abraham. Few seventh-century Christians would have been aware of that common ground. But there were, and there still are, fundamental differences between Islam and Christianity. Dr Mashuq Ally, Lecturer in Religious Studies at St David's University College, Lampeter, says that a basic dogmatic difference which must be recognised is that whereas Christians hold Jesus as being the Son of God and therefore God, this has no place in Islam. Jesus is much revered in the Koran and by Muslims, and in fact not to accept him would mean that you would not be a Muslim. But the perception that Muslims have of Jesus is very different from the Christian perception. For the Muslim, Jesus is a prophet, a human being like everyone else, continuing the same message that Moses and Abraham had given to humanity and which the prophet Mohammed continued.

In the East, inevitably, Islam had its effect on the power balance

The Night Ride to Heaven – the ascent of the prophet Mohammed on Buraq, a human-faced donkey mule

within Christianity. Dr Judith Herrin, Visiting Professor at Princeton University in America, says that in the course of the seventh century the patriarchates of Alexandria, Antioch and Jerusalem were overrun by the forces of Islam. Although the patriarchs continued to reside there and to control their Christian populations, many people converted to Islam. The invading forces did not make it a condition by any means – in fact they rather wished that their subject peoples would retain their own faith and pay a higher tax. But a great many people clearly slipped from Christianity into Islam, and the patriarchates – those three Eastern patriarchates which had been very important centres of Christian control and organisation – diminished in stature, leaving Constantinople unrivalled in the leadership of Eastern Christians.

Islam cleared the board for future power struggles between the Church of the West based in Rome and the Church of the East based in Constantinople. The invasion of Palestine would eventually induce the Crusades. Already the holy places had a special hold over the minds of all Christian believers. Bede records in detail descriptions of Jerusalem, Bethlehem and Hebron. Caedmon, the illiterate cowherd turned poet under the tutelage of Hilda, sings of creation and also of the great events of Jesus's life which took place in Jerusalem.

Caedmon's fame is intertwined with Hilda's. Sister Benedicta Ward says he was a cowherd on the lands of Hilda. Every night the servants met for a drink. They would sit round in the hall in the servants' quarters and pass round the harp to sing songs. Caedmon could not sing and Sister Benedicta says that he was very ashamed of himself for not being able to. He hated it and the moment he saw the harp approaching he used to get up and go out and sulk. One night he went out and lay down with the cows, hating the whole thing, and dreamt that someone stood by him and said, 'Caedmon, sing to me.' And he said, 'I can't sing.' And the someone said, 'Sing about the principal of all creation.'

Caedmon found in his sleep that he could sing, and when he woke up, he went to the manager of the servants who took him to Hilda and to everyone's surprise he could still sing. Then she decided to have him trained. But first, she had him examined, not by the good men, but by the clever men – the poets and the bards who knew about metre and verse. She wanted to see if Caedmon was really a poet and he was, so she had him very carefully trained in the scriptures and he began to put them into Anglo-Saxon verse. It is, Sister Benedicta thinks, a very remarkable story, especially as Anglo-Saxon had not been a written language for that long and suddenly here was this boy from the backwoods producing quite outstandingly beautiful Anglo-Saxon poetry which was written down, though sadly all but lost.

Hilda's patronage of Caedmon points to a resolution of an anomaly in the life of the Church in Britain. Dr Nelson thinks that all the evidence we have is that the first people the missionaries went for were nobles, kings and queens. The first people who were converted belonged to that class. Hilda's career is important because in some way she is a bridge from that class to humbler people. The story that Bede tells about her and Caedmon, the servant, the illiterate, who nevertheless by divine inspiration transmits an authentically Christian message through his songs, which she then approves of and which are then sung in a public place which she presides over, is a bridge between the literate, élite culture and a humbler reception of Christianity. It is the nearest we can get to understanding how Christianity straddled that gap in the course of the seventh century.

Sister Benedicta finds Hilda impressive partly because of her northernness, and partly because of her deep concern with education. She was a very learned woman and the school at Whitby was very fine and influential. There is an interesting contrast, between thirty-three years as an Anglo-Saxon princess with all the beautiful trappings of royalty at Sutton Hoo, and then Whitby on a headland, an isolated monastery, cold and bare, austere, as a monastery should be. Hilda, she says, is one of the supreme examples of how absolutely unnecessary it was for a woman to be a priest since Hilda attained a position of considerable authority within the Church without ever seeking ordination.

For Dr Nelson, Hilda of Whitby's life was not one of monastic withdrawal. She had chosen an active path which many others throughout the Middle Ages would follow. She thinks she must have been a woman of tremendous personal authority, perhaps ambitious. She did not want to go to a Frankish monastery, only to withdraw from the world. She was a woman, like many others in the Middle Ages, who seized the opportunity that the Church held out to women, of exercising spiritual authority in an ecclesiastical role. The role of abbess was a unique opportunity for women of high status to exercise power in an approved way, and Hilda seized that opportunity and in so doing left her mark on her century.

A FRANKISH DAVID

.

Nearly one hundred years after the death of Hilda of Whitby, but before the last glimmers of Northumbria's golden age of faith and learning had been shattered by the Viking axe, a humiliating defeat was sustained by a homeward-bound army, ambushed by Gascons in the Pyrenees. Later the scene of the battle would be remembered as Roncesvalles but contemporary sources spend two or three sentences on it and do not even dignify it with a name. In centuries to come the story would be transformed. The Gascons would become Saracens. All that was most noble and all that was most fearful about the eighth century – the dream of chivalry and the terror of encroaching Islam – could be invoked by recalling the dying notes of an ivory horn blown by Roland, commander of the Breton march, ambushed and facing sure defeat at Roncesvalles.

> *In the dire pain Count Roland blows his horn of ivory, as the battle nears its close. Bright blood gushes from his mouth. His head is wounded piteously. Across the hills and valleys the emperor hears the horn's lament. He says, 'Take your arms Christian knights and cry your battle shout. Do you not hear Roland's call?' To answer Roland's call the emperor has commanded that his trumpets be sounded. In great anger he rides on that Roland may not die. High are the hills and deep the valleys. Too long delayed the ivory blast. Count Roland lies dying. With his last strength he turns his face towards the Saracens so that the king, his emperor and sweet liege lord, will know that he died unafraid of the foe.*

The twelfth-century *Song of Roland* is a story of Christian heroism pitted against the feared and barely understood armies of Islam. It was a popular song, sung in one of its earlier forms by William the Conqueror's men on their way to Hastings in 1066. The battle details in the *Song of Roland* are undiluted fantasy but the sweet liege lord who occupies Roland's last thoughts was very much flesh and blood. He was Charles the squeaky-voiced, the bastard son of Pepin the Short. History remembers him as Charles the Great – Charlemagne, the first Holy Roman emperor, the architect of Europe, the protector of learning, the backbone of the papacy and the defender of Christendom.

Charlemagne was born into the middle of the eighth century – a

A reliquary of Charlemagne, the first Holy Roman Emperor – a good swimmer, he found writing tricky

century which was not for faint hearts. In the East it was a time of iconoclasm, sieges, religious tumult and political uncertainty. Irene the empress failed to live up to her peaceful name. She mutilated and murdered her own son to secure power. In the West the Arabs swept through, halted only by the Frankish Charles Martel. It was a time of ecclesiastical fraud, learning and martyrdom. In Holland Boniface, the Devon man who cut down the sacred oak of Thor, was put to the sword. In Rome a pope was beaten up and a clumsy attempt made to remove his eyes and tongue.

This was Charlemagne's world. He not only survived it, he also controlled a large part of it and moulded its legacy to all future centuries including our own. Charlemagne was in many ways a larger-than-life character. His stature grew after his death. Early medieval writers claim he was eight feet tall – or at least eight times the size of his feet, but perhaps he had small feet. His beard was a foot long. He was solidly built and had sparkling eyes. He could eat a whole goose at one sitting and could lift a fully-armed knight with one hand. More credibly he was a family man who loved company.

Russell Chamberlain, author and biographer of Charlemagne, says that he was enormously human. He loved having people round with him. He did not like banquets, but there were great family tables where everybody turned up, where he would personally carve and heap people's plates high. He had four or five wives and an uncounted number of mistresses – so many that there was considerable confusion in European genealogy for the next five or six hundred years, as this or that princeling would bob up and claim to have Carolingian blood, no matter how diluted, no matter how legitimate. He had countless illegitimate children.

His relationship with his daughters was most curious. He had four or five and they were all most beautiful, but he would not allow any of them to marry. He was quite prepared and quite happy if they had illegitimate children. The palace was swarming with them – all came under the great warm embraces of Charlemagne – but his refusal to let his daughters marry is the one unsavoury area about his character.

Away from home, Charlemagne was a fighter. He led fifty-three campaigns across Europe – from Greece to Brittany and from Spain to Denmark, but he was more than a warrior king. He listened, he took advice, and he considered his words. Thick-necked and thick-skinned, he was a complex man. As well as his numerous wives, mistresses, and concubines, he also kept a pet elephant. He enjoyed hunting, particularly bison, but he also took a great interest in the liturgy and Church reform and he was keen on the *Rule* of St Benedict. An enthusiastic, if brutal, missionary, he bludgeoned the Saxons into Christianity.

He found writing tricky and was much better at swimming. Yet he delighted in the company of learned men. His favourite book was St Augustine's *City of God* – but had he read it or was it read to him? Was the first Holy Roman emperor illiterate? Dr Rosamund McKitterick, Fellow of Newnham College, Cambridge, says that it is pretty certain he could read, but writing was a different matter. Einhardt, the royal biographer, tells us that Charlemagne did try to learn to write but found it hard. He used to get up in the middle of the night when he could not sleep, find a pen and have another go. That seems to point to someone who could barely form his letters but Dr McKitterick thinks it might mean that what Charlemagne was attempting to write was the new Carolingian minuscule, which was a very regular style of handwriting with separated letters and quite difficult. Whereas Charlemagne, if he had learned to write at all as part of the administrative training he may have received as a young man, would have written rather a nasty cursive joined-up scrawl.

He appears to have encouraged scholarship and possessed some wonderful illuminated books specifically written for him. They are exactly what you would expect a Christian king to own. They are grand gospel books, plastered with gold, written on purple vellum with intricate illustrations and elaborate script. We also have evidence of the extent of his library which was obviously an inspiration to scholars.

Charlemagne had contacts beyond Europe. He kept up a correspondence with Harun al Rashid, the caliph of Baghdad, from whom he received a tent, a waterclock, and the keys of the Holy Sepulchre. His contacts with Constantinople proved to be less fruitful. Inevitably the emperors there, who considered themselves the heirs to the Roman empire, would be less than impressed by a royal dynasty barely two generations old laying claim to the title of 'Roman emperor', whether holy or not. Throughout the first half of the eighth century Constantinople had been racked by the controversy of the iconoclasts or image breakers, expressing an unease as old as the Mosaic commandment against graven images – a prohibition recently reinforced by Mohammed, the holy one of Mecca.

Dr Judith Herrin believes that iconoclasm may have been sparked off by a spate of Muslim destruction of Christian images in the caliphate in the 720s AD. It did have its immediate reaction in the Byzantine territories under the control of the patriarch of Constantinople but in the West the practice of image veneration was not widely developed. In Rome itself the images were cherished and were not taken down in accordance with the imperial edict to remove all statues and images. So in Rome, where there were large communities of Greek monks, there was a tremendous rallying to the holy icons. Indeed in the course of the eighth century we can trace the promotion of image veneration in Rome and a positively Greek and Byzantine influence in that trend brought by refugees from the iconoclastic persecution in Constantinople.

John of Damascus, known as Chrysorrhoas (the gold-pouring) on account of his eloquence, and revered as the last of the Church Fathers, lived out his entire life under Moslem rule. He was a staunch defender of icons in the face of the campaign waged by the Eastern emperor Leo III. Professor Anthony Bryer says that iconoclasm is the only great heresy imposed from above. When Leo smashed the icons, the chroniclers at the time said it was because of a Jewish plot. Or because Santorini had erupted. But there were several reasons. To some extent the emperor was trying to get hold of his own Church. The popular Church, as you might call it, the monastic Church, the Church which venerated icons and which used icons, was to some extent outside his grasp. The state Church was faced with these very dangerous, almost revolutionary monks – people who were social drop-outs who broke all the rules and who did not belong to the system, but who held the hearts and minds of the faithful. They were themselves, in a sense, living icons and had great power. They, like icons, were intermediaries between the ghastly world on earth and the kingdom of God. They were intermediaries between the peasant and the state. They could be fools for Christ – they could go and tell the emperor what they thought of him without any fear. They were intercessors, just like icons.

Constantinople was a nervous city. Faith in icons had not saved it from the indignity of siege in 718 when Moslem armies surrounded the city. The siege was broken, but Leo spent the next twelve years repulsing Arab advances in Asia Minor and managing to tilt the balance of power in his favour. Others adopted less orthodox tactics in the power game. In the West, when Pepin the Short, Charlemagne's father, was anointed king of the Franks, he made sure the last of the long-haired, do-nothing Merovingian kings, Childeric III, had a haircut and was deposited in a monastery. The pope was having trouble with the Lombards in Italy. He and Pepin entered into an alliance of mutual benefit. And at about this time a decidedly bent ecclesiastical card was brought into play, a document called the Donation of Constantine. This forgery which carried weight

The Donation of Constantine – a widely believed fiction which held currency for more than a thousand years

DEVS SE TIBI TV TE DEO.

Pepin the Short, king of the Franks and father of Charlemagne. Pepin, who more than made up for his lack of inches by his shrewd, political sense, ensured that the last of the long-haired, do-nothing Merovingian kings was deposed and given a haircut

until the fifteenth century claimed that pope Silvester, who had been pope during the reign of Constantine, had cured Constantine of leprosy and had received in return from a grateful emperor the imperial diadem, and jurisdiction over Rome, Italy and the Western provinces. Pepin invaded

Italy and the Lombard king was forced to surrender twenty-two cities and castles to the pope. With Pepin's military muscle the myth of the Donation of Constantine was beginning to become a reality and would remain one for well over a thousand years.

Pepin had another ally, Boniface the holy man from Crediton in Devon, who had played an important part in Pepin's coronation. Boniface, with many German converts to his credit, could offer Pepin a framework of authority through which to reform the Frankish church. Boniface pulled the Frankish church together and then he and his English monks set off north again.

Boniface and his followers had crossed the channel in the first place, Dr Jinty Nelson believes, not to reform Christians but to convert pagans. The English seemed to have a sense that they were one people with the Saxons back in Germany and they saw it as almost a family obligation to bring the Saxons on the Continent to Christ. What the missionaries gave to all their people under Frankish rule was a sense of identity as a Christian people. Had the Franks just asserted their imperial rule without that kind of ideological backing, it would have been seen as an affront by Bavarians, Thuringians and Saxons. Because it was packaged in Christianity it became acceptable. But it was not just the packaging, it was a perfectly genuine assertion that Christianity transcended these differences between peoples. They were different peoples, but they were not different races. The Saxons and the Franks felt themselves to be very different from each other and Christianity was the uniting factor. Charlemagne was trying to create a union of France and Germany. The German component was only integrated into that Frankish empire through Christianity. This is what Boniface's missionary work made possible.

Charlemagne was a child when Boniface was killed. The man who tempted the wrath of Thor was killed by the German tribesmen he loved while he was sitting in his tent reading. Other Englishmen would follow in Boniface's footsteps. Some would end up in Charlemagne's court after Pepin died in 767 but Charlemagne was not all that far removed from the heathen tribes Boniface had died among.

The Reverend Michael Smith says that Charlemagne was still very much a barbarian, but he was one who had begun to see there was a certain amount of point in Christianity. Rather like Constantine before him, Charlemagne was no intellectual, but his heart was in the right place. He wanted to learn and to get things right. Deep down he was mortally afraid that if he did not get things right with God perhaps his empire would fall apart. He also had a very keen sense that he was a newcomer. He and the mayors of the palace before him had taken over from the weak Merovingian kings and they had got there purely by the strength of their strong right arms. He felt very much that he needed some spiritual help and, while he was not a great scholar himself, he was a good collector of other people. He organised a very effective brain drain. He pinched Alcuin from the cathedral school at York, he took Paul the deacon from Lombardy, he had various scholars from Ireland, and Theodolph from Orleans. He gathered this group at his court and he set off from there.

Charlemagne was not an academic but he was an enthusiast. He longed, he said, to have at court twelve scholars as great as Jerome and Augustine. Alcuin of York the great book ferreter mildly rebuked him, telling him that since God had only provided two minds of that calibre in the entire history of the Church, it was unlikely that he would be able to gather twelve for his court. Alcuin the deacon, an unambitious man who hated hurrying, did what he could. He educated Charlemagne and his courtiers by means of question and answer. Knowledge became a fascinating campaign, and it was not all serious. There were nicknames with biblical or scholarly allusion. Charlemagne was David the golden king. Theodolph of Orleans was the soaring poet Pindar, Angilbert was Homer. And Alcuin? He was Flaccus, named after Horace the most accessible of classical poets.

Alcuin the Englishman occupied a rare position of privilege in Charlemagne's court. But did he achieve anything solid? The Reverend Kenneth Stevenson, author and liturgist, says that the genius of Alcuin was that he was an adapter. He was very good at taking up other people's ideas and he was very keen on the early Church Fathers. He has been credited with writing many prayers and one prayer still used every week in the Church of England, *Almighty God to whom all hearts are open*, was written by him. He emerged at the end of the eighth century as a key figure in Charlemagne's Church policy. Alcuin was the teacher and Charlemagne was the pupil, but Charlemagne saw to it that he kept on top the whole time. There was an intimate relationship between them and even after Alcuin had finished helping Charlemagne in the Palatine school in Aachen and had become abbot of Tours, they still corresponded and they even had rows. Remember it was he who began calling Charlemagne David and that in a sense was quite a serious joke because it epitomised the pretentiousness of Charlemagne's empire – that he was a king of a new and expanding kingdom and that he wanted to be intimately con-nected with the Church. In the chapel at Aachen, which is now the cathedral, there is a big throne which is not the bishop's throne but Charlemagne's chair from which he presided at services. He did not perform liturgical functions, but he used to sit there, and if the lesson was too long, he would bang his stick on the floor to stop it. There was no doubt that he felt he was ultimately in charge.

Throughout the time Alcuin was at court Charlemagne conducted a running battle against the pagan Saxons. He tried to convert them to Christianity by force. He outlawed paganism. Eating meat in Lent became a capital offence. The Saxons rebelled and four and a half thousand of them were massacred in a single day. How could Charlemagne reconcile such action with being a Christian monarch? As Dr McKitterick says, he presumably thought that it was for their own good and that they would go to hell, if they did not go over to Christianity. But there is no actual specific statement that he was trying to save their souls. If you were a Saxon you would have hated his guts and they did. There are the famous Saxon decrees which read: if you will not accept baptism then you will be beheaded; if you offend a priest then the penalty is death; if you desecrate a church the penalty is death – on and on and on. When he heard about this Alcuin was so alarmed that he wrote admonishing the king, saying you cannot force people into Christianity.

The same Charlemagne who was laying into the Saxons was also legislating for church life. All the bishops, most of the major abbots and many priests in his kingdom would receive a royal present at their consecration, a book written by St Gregory on pastoral care. Charlemagne had already decided the monastery he would like to die in. He legislated for the morals of the clergy but did not feel at all bound to one wife. Was he a hypocrite or was he genuinely religious? The Reverend Kenneth Stevenson thinks you would have to be very cynical to say that it was simply a power game. He was a very devout person. He said his prayers regularly. He went to church several times every day if he could. You have only to look at the legacy throughout the empire and see the amount of growth and development at the end of that eighth century to see the fruits of his work. Some people today say that all the problems of modern Europe – Church and state – began in that century, but that is too cynical.

Whatever his faults, Charlemagne was mild when compared to the Eastern empress Irene. At one stage there was some speculation that there might be a marriage alliance. It came to nothing. A lucky escape for Charlemagne. Dr McKitterick says that Irene comes over as rather a ghastly female who thought nothing of putting her son's eyes out, but there is no doubt that she was of singular ability and strength of mind, with strong views on subjects and prepared to act on them.

On a church level, relations between Rome and Constantinople were reasonably good at this time. The papacy's problems lay closer to home. As Italy fell under Frankish rule, safeguards were invented to prevent the pope becoming little more than a political nominee. From 769 onwards it was decided that no layman, no matter how exalted, could play any part in the choice of bishop of Rome. But once elected it was inevitable that

The coronation of the Byzantine empress Irene. Once a prospective marriage partner for Charlemagne, she blinded and murdered her own son to secure power

the paths of pope and king would become intertwined. In 795 Leo, the head of the papal treasury, was unanimously elected pope. He immediately sought Charlemagne's patronage. An astute move. Before long, Leo was severely beaten up by a gang supporting the previous pope's nephew as candidate to the Holy See. The report said his eyes were gouged out and his tongue ripped out. Notker Balbulus, in the *Deeds of Charlemagne*, records that his eyelids were slashed across and healed, leaving a thin red line which lasted for the rest of his life. More dead than alive, Leo was smuggled out of Rome and fled to Charlemagne's court.

On Christmas Day 800 Leo and Charlemagne were both in Rome. Charlemagne went to Mass at St Peter's. It was one of the few occasions when he was not wearing Frankish dress. In the course of the Mass an apparently spontaneous event took place which would change the course of the history. Leo, miraculously recovered, placed a crown upon Charlemagne's allegedly unsuspecting head. The coronation of the first Holy Roman emperor had taken place.

Professor Donald Bullough, Professor of Medieval History at St Andrews University, Scotland, believes there was method and rehearsal behind the spontaneity. There was, he says, a certain amount of kidding going on. No one would believe now that Leo had lost his tongue, literally, and then recovered his voice, even if he might have suffered a severe shock in what seems to have been a kind of mugging. Obviously there had been discussions going on for some time about whether it was appropriate to enhance Charlemagne's position as king of the Franks. And it is most improbable that there had not been extensive discussions about how this might be done. It is likely that the ceremony on Christmas Day 800, which was what people call the Coronation of Charlemagne, or the Imperial Coronation, had been planned and rehearsed. Or it may be that what really happened was one person stealing a march on the other. Leo was putting himself at the centre of the ceremony by putting a crown on Charlemagne's head.

Charlemagne grew into the majesty of his new title, but it must be remembered that the Holy Roman empire bore scant resemblance to the old empire which was held together by law. The new empire was held together by faith. Difficult though it may seem to reconcile with his treatment of the Saxons, Charlemagne, the Holy Roman emperor, genuinely believed that he was responsible for the faith of his subjects. The loyalty he exacted from all his male subjects was one of adherence to the service of God. It was almost apologetically explained that the oath was

necessary because the emperor did not have time to pay adequate attention to every one of his subjects. This was a new idea. But the staples of the imperial administration – tax, the army and the bureaucracy – were missing.

Dr Jinty Nelson thinks this was both a strength and a weakness. Politically the Carolingian empire lasted for at the most three generations. But it was much longer lasting than the Roman empire in an ideological sense, because Christianity could survive the collapse of the empire which protected it. The structures of the Church and the Church's law, and it does have a law however many people disregard it, gave Christianity a permanence which the Roman empire had lacked. The culture of the Roman empire had been too much associated with its institutions and when they fell its culture also fell. But Christianity survived the fall of the Carolingian empire.

The weaknesses of the Holy Roman empire are well documented. Russell Chamberlain also believes it had hidden strengths. The standard jibe against it is that it is neither holy, nor Roman, nor an empire, and that is true, but like all jibes, it misses the central point. The theme was deeply noble – the idea of a priest and a warrior together ruling all Christians.

Charlemagne's coronation has been seen as an instance of the Church dominating the State. In reality, Charlemagne did not feel beholden to the papacy. The political legacy of the Holy Roman empire was to have repercussions far beyond the next century. Charlemagne invented modern Europe, for, as Dr Nelson says, Europe had not been a unity before. Contemporaries saw Charlemagne as creating this unity and it was con- temporaries of Charlemagne who used that word, Europe, for the first time since antiquity. What made this new Europe was Christianity. It was a shared set of institutions, so that you would know wherever you went within Christendom what a monastery looked like, the kind of liturgical observances that would go on in that monastery, all conducted in a single religious language – Latin. It was a unity of observance. It was also asserting a unity of belief, a belief in a particular deity which excluded others. Christianity was drawing boundaries between us, the chosen ones, and them outside. That was very important in forming an identity.

Charlemagne's coronation revived the idea of a holy god-given kingship, a king under God like the kings of the children of Israel. Alcuin's nickname for Charlemagne was prophetic. When the 'Frankish David' felt death was approaching he crowned his own son as successor. He spent his last days in prayer and almsgiving, according to some. Others say he went hunting. Perhaps he did both. But what was the lasting achievement of Charlemagne, the Frankish warlord who had found writing difficult?

The Council of Nicea – Arius the heretic is inset beneath

Opposite top: St Jerome the Westerner, a hermit in a decidedly eastern setting

Opposite bottom: In this painting by Raphael, Leo I halts invasion by Attila with the help of an airborne St Peter and St Paul

Above: The last conversation of Benedict and Scholastica. Benedict is protesting he must leave and Scholastica is pulling a theological fast one by praying for him to stay. The monk on the left has spotted the first signs of rain

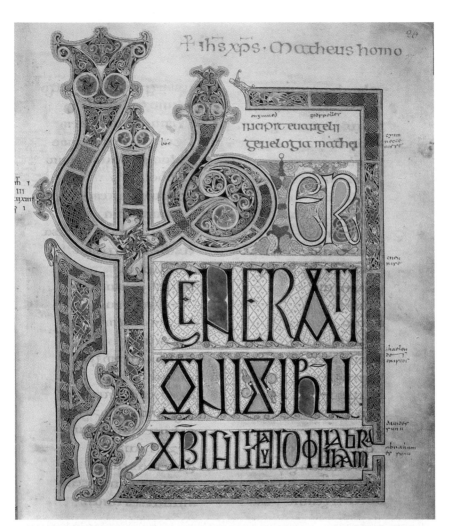

Opposite top: The first page of the gospel of St Matthew from the Lindisfarne Gospels

Opposite bottom: Charlemagne is crowned by a pale-looking Leo III

Left: Kasia, the sharp-tongued abbess, holding the text of her hymn which is still sung in Greek orthodox churches every Holy Week. At her feet lies the golden apple of Theophilus the Unfortunate

Below: St Dunstan robed as archbishop – a position he would never have attained but for a youthful illness which made him drop his more secular career plans

Top: The Conquest of Jerusalem – what had begun as a knightly ideal ended in brutality and carnage

Bottom: St Hildegard the prophet of the green movement, (bottom left), and her vision of the richness of the earth and its seasons

Opposite: St Francis of Assisi, showing the marks of the stigmata on his hands and sides

Dante (School of Giotto) – *his contemporaries believed that you could see he had been burnt by the fires of hell*

Professor Bullough says he brought the last major Germanic people, the Saxons, together with some non-Germanic peoples like the nomadic Avars in the area of eastern Austria and Hungary, within the Christian orbit, and they were subsequently extremely grateful to him, though they had resisted him so stoutly. He raised the whole level of cultural activity: the building up of libraries in monasteries and cathedral churches is a spectacular development in his later years. And he raised the whole level of literacy, particularly, though by no means exclusively, Latin learning. It was never to sink as low again, not even in the worst days of the tenth century.

Charlemagne's story has been layered with romance and legend. Was the man beneath it all a hero, and specifically a Christian hero? Russell Chamberlain thinks so. We can look upon him, he says, as the last of the Romans or the first of the Europeans. He had a genuine vision of the United States of Europe – the European empire. The Carolingian empire was the last attempt for Europe to work together as one people – a nation. After his death, the West plunges into the so-called Dark Ages. His monument was a dream but a dream which lingers still.

A GOLDEN APPLE FROM
THE EMPEROR

·

Some fifteen years after all Europe, from the rising to the setting sun according to a monk of Bobbio, had echoed with the laments of men, women and children mourning the death of Charlemagne, in the East Theophilus, known as the Unfortunate because of his military record, decided it was time to find a wife. According to one tradition he made his decision in a quaint way.

> *The daughters of all the principal families of Constantinople were summoned to the imperial palace. In the appointed room, the young women assembled and were drawn up in two silent lines. The emperor Theophilus entered carrying a golden apple. As he slowly inspected the lines, the beauty of one of the young women caught his eye. Suddenly tongue-tied, Theophilus cast round for something to say. He lamely observed to her that women were the source of much evil. She quickly retorted that they were also the source of much good. Displeased, the emperor passed on.*

The story continues that Theophilus gave the apple and the title of empress to Theodora, whose wordlessness he found much more pleasing. The talkative young woman was called Kasia. After the imperial slight Kasia sought religious seclusion but not obscurity. Her writing and evidence of her sharp tongue survive to this day. Every year she is remembered in the liturgy of the Greek Orthodox Church.

Kasia of Byzantium – wit, epigrammatist, hymn-writer, poet and abbess – lived through the first three quarters of the ninth century. Byzantium, or Constantinople, still considered itself the heir of the old Roman empire. Rome might have fallen, but the Roman empire of the East had not. But this Roman empire was entirely Greek in culture. Their law was Roman but it was translated into Greek. There was no knowledge of Latin. Those who called themselves the successors of Augustus and Constantine needed interpreters if they wanted to talk to the Romans of the West.

In the West, it was a time of disaster. In the short term Charlemagne's legacy of a Holy Roman empire bore only empty, withered fruit. Europe was battered by Magyars, Vikings and Saracens. In the first half of the ninth century the papacy was successively buffeted by the threat of Saracen

Kasia of Byzantium. Wit, epigrammatist, iconodule, poet and abbess – but not empress

seaborne invasion and the complications of both Frankish and Byzantine imperial love affairs. Towards the end of the century the papacy itself was the problem.

In the East, the story was very different. It was a time of revival and enthusiasm. These years more than any others since apostolic times have left their stamp on Orthodox Christianity. It was a time of vitality, of hidden agendas, of incest, of missionary rivalry, of pious empresses and sacrilegious emperors, of anger and holiness.

This was Kasia's world. The historical Kasia had one thing in common with the demure Theodora who became empress. They were both ardent iconodules, that is to say they firmly believed in using icons as part of Christian life and worship. And the sharpness with which Kasia opposed the iconoclasts who condemned icons as idolatrous is a link, Andrew Louth, Senior Lecturer in Religious Studies at Goldsmiths' College, London, believes, between the Kasia of imperial legend and Kasia the historical abbess. Three letters were written to her by St Theodore of Studion, the great monastic reformer in Constantinople, who was prominent as a supporter of the veneration of icons. In the letters, Kasia, a young woman in her twenties, comes over as a rather intolerant supporter of the veneration of icons and intolerant of those who were less certain than herself. She made sure that one of the iconodules, who wavered and joined the iconoclast movement, came in for harsh treatment by ensuring that he did not see the sacraments on his death-bed. Theodore of Studion reproved her for this.

Kasia threw herself into the iconoclast controversy with enthusiasm. In theory, iconoclasm should have disappeared once and for all in 787 when the seventh ecumenical council came down unequivocally on the side of icons. But mistrust of icons lingered among a small influential group of people – the old military families who had political muscle if not theological insight. A run of military failure persuaded them that God was not on the side of the icons. While Kasia was growing up under Theophilus' predecessor, Leo, iconoclasm was once again imperial policy. It was at this time that Theodore of Studion was imprisoned for his support of the icons. Several leading churchmen were deposed and Nicephorus, the pro-icon patriarch, was removed from office by the emperor and put behind bars.

The Byzantium which Kasia would have known as a young woman was alive with political intrigue, always tempered by religious considerations. Leo V decided to kill Michael his rival by having him burnt alive in the furnace which heated the water for the public bath. He delayed the deed because he did not want to sully the feast of Christmas. His piety proved fatal. Michael had him hacked to death while singing matins in the imperial chapel.

In Byzantium the emperors retained the major say in the appointment of patriarchs. It was impossible to separate religion from politics or politics from religion. This was a fact of Byzantine daily life and not only of imperial daily life. Nigel Wilson, Fellow of Lincoln College, Oxford, says that it was a society with a kind of religious mania. The old story that if you went out shopping in Constantinople and went to the market to buy fish, you could not complete your transaction without having an argument with the fishmonger about the nature of the Trinity as you collected the change still held true. And you can see the religious mania coming out in the iconoclastic controversy. There is much reference in Orthodox writers to their opponents but the language they use is simply vitriolic abuse. It is very hard to find out what the iconoclasts actually thought. It is just a torrent of the most foul-mouthed insults, which does indicate that there was a real streak of religious intolerance in the population at large.

After Leo's dramatic death iconoclasm lay dormant for about fifteen years. Then, towards the end of Theophilus' reign, John Grammaticus the iconoclast became patriarch. Never one to mince words he believed that all those who spoke in favour of icons should be put to death or sent into exile. The iconodules would not keep silent. They maintained that the Old Testament strictures against graven images no longer applied. Once again the arguments of John of Damascus, John the Gold-pourer, were used. Kallistos Ware, Bishop of the Greek Orthodox Church, says that the defence given by John of Damascus was above all an appeal to the incarnation. God in himself cannot be depicted – no one has ever seen God – you should not show God the Father as an old man with a beard. Therefore, says John of Damascus, it is perfectly understandable that in the Old Testament period no images of God were allowed. But the incarnation has changed all that, and since the word has been made flesh and become truly human, we can make an icon of Christ, who is the human face of God. Supporters of the icons would go a step further. They would say it is not only possible to make icons, it is essential. If you refuse to make icons of Christ, if you refuse to depict him, that suggests that his body is somehow unreal, illusory. So icons safeguard the full reality of the incarnation.

Behold the woman fallen in many sins is a hymn written by Kasia about the woman who anointed Jesus' feet, which is sung in Greek Orthodox Churches every Holy Week. The hymn is inward-looking and humble, begging forgiveness and certain of God's mercy. But there was another side to Kasia's writing. According to Andrew Louth, Kasia's secular poems are rather different. Some of them are about subjects like friendship. Others are satirical. There is one striking poem in which every line begins with the same word *miso,* I hate. There is another series about the life of the monk. But Kasia is not in any way cynical. She has genuine ideals that she cherishes, and which she thinks should be fulfilled.

Kasia has a low toleration threshold of fools or hypocrites. She had founded her own monastery at a time when Theodore of Studion was revising and restoring the Eastern monastic rule by going back to the earliest manuscripts of St Basil. Throughout the Byzantine empire monasteries like Kasia's were iconodule strongholds. Undoubtedly part of the imperial iconoclast policies was prompted by unease at the growing wealth of monasteries. Economic independence, then as now, can breed political independence. This was part, but only part, of the reason for the iconoclasts' hostility to icons.

Dr Judith Herrin says that for centuries the saints, as well as Christ and his mother, had been portrayed in images. At the Council of 691 a canon had established that Christ should not be represented as the Lamb of God but should be shown in his full human form, and this encouraged the representation of Christ not only in images, but also on the imperial gold coinage. Such things bring a portrait likeness of the holiest people into the lives of ordinary people and give them a much more direct contact with the godhead and with the representatives of God as they are recorded in the Gospels. But where people feel they can communicate directly with God, through these painted images, there is a danger that they will ignore

Theodora, the ardent iconodule whose demure silence won her the imperial golden apple

the liturgical services conducted by priests, and that they will reduce their commitment to the spiritual values of Christianity as a whole. This is the point at which we can see that the question of idolatry may arise.

One of the things which is very much debated is whether ordinary people, while they shared a view that the holy icons could indeed intercede for men and women with God, also realised that, where their prayers had not been answered, there was some failure of the images to deliver. In the terror and suffering caused by the Arab raids of the seventh and early eighth centuries, we get a glimpse in the sources of the great anguish suffered by ordinary people who put their faith in the holy icons and their local saints to protect them from these fearsome invaders and were then deceived. And where the faith has been so deep and the commitment so great, the disappointment means that people react very strongly. They condemn the icons as worthless and turn against them. This is what we see very clearly among certain populations of the Eastern empire whose lands and farms and towns were ravaged, not just on one occasion, but annually from the late seventh century onwards, by raiding armies of Muslims anxious to conquer Constantinople and unconcerned for the loss of life of Christians in their way.

The iconoclast controversy did little to strengthen the Church in the East or to improve relations between Rome and Constantinople. It finally came to an end in 842 when Theophilus died and Theodora, acting as regent for her son Michael, reinstated the icons to their full position of honour. Bishop Kallistos says that this triumph of Orthodoxy which we could date to 842–843 is certainly the most important single event in ninth-century Orthodox Christianity. It represents the final end of the iconoclast controversy, but it represents much more than that. It also represents an end to the early Byzantine stage in Church history. There is a feeling from the middle of the ninth century onwards that the main lines of the Christian faith – faith in the Holy Trinity, in the person of Christ, in the holy icons – have been laid down once for all. That does not mean that there is no creative development at a later stage – but there is none the less a sense that doctrine is somehow a rounded and completed whole, and the triumph of Orthodoxy sets the seal on that.

After the resolution of the iconoclast controversy, Theodora continued to rule soberly and prudently on behalf of her son, Michael III. After thirteen years she stepped down in his favour, and he soon acquired a considerable reputation for ingenious sacrilege. He is credited with grave-robbing, with dressing up in archbishop's vestments and with serving his own brand of Holy Communion – a poisonous mixture of mustard and vinegar. His antics were known in Byzantium but not elsewhere, so when Ratislav, the ruler of Moravia, an area corresponding

Christ attended by St Cyril the alphabet-maker and St Methodius, the much conspired against monk. One a former diplomat, the other a military officer turned monk, they gave Europe a third international language

roughly to modern Czechoslovakia or western Hungary, decided he wanted to know more about Christianity he sent an embassy to Michael III asking for a teacher capable of teaching the Slavs in their own language.

Two teachers were sent, the brothers Cyril and Methodius. They would create a new written language. As Cyril Mango, Professor of Byzantine and Modern Greek at Oxford University, says, Cyril and Methodius, who knew Slavonic because they had been born in Thessalonika where people spoke Slavonic, insisted on spreading the word of God and celebrating the liturgy in the vernacular. This is something that was not always done. The Church of Rome was against it normally but somehow or other the two brothers started translating certain books of the Bible, the Psalter, the New Testament and the Liturgy, in order to help to convert the Moravians. If they had been sent to a less distant land, such as Bulgaria which was on the doorstep of the Empire, perhaps the Byzantines would not have been so keen to give them their own culture and vernacular.

Cyril invented the Glagolitic alphabet for the Slavs and he or his pupils composed the Cyrillic alphabet which is used today throughout the Soviet Union. Cyril was used to foreign assignments. He had already been sent on a diplomatic mission to the Caliph Mutawakhil. With his brother Methodius, a former military officer turned monk, he had also visited the Khazars of the Crimea. A few years after that journey both Cyril and

тѵоренаго ОБРАЗА та ншего і҃ѵ х҃а ѿ
Едеса въкостантиньграе ѵ҃ доуг мн
ѳ҃i тѵы м҃никъ Флра йла вра. ѣѵдоуг ѯг.
і҃е ртѣнесеніемощемь стго а҃пла варѳо
ломеа , йстгоа҃пла титта ѣѵма г҃ аі.
к҃ѳ оѵѣкновеніе чтныа главы іоанна
кртла. наур прогла д҃, возвелитисе
праведникъ ѿ оуслышнѣ тьмой воса
а҃ коды ѵма г҃ из, наур. ѵма кд, по
ложеніе чтнаго пойаса прѣстыи б҃це,
ѣѵдіе оугла д҃: КОНЕЦЬ б҃ім м҃це.:

A Cyrillic manuscript — part of the legacy of Cyril the precedent-breaking apostle of the Slavs

Methodius had become priests. They were the ideal candidates for the Moravian mission and ideal ambassadors for Byzantium.

Sir Dimitri Obolensky, Fellow in Byzantine and East European History, Christ Church, Oxford, says that we know that Cyril was very proud to belong to the Byzantine cultural élite, and in other earlier missions abroad we find him very conscious of the fact that he represented the most civilised state on earth, the Byzantine empire. We know a little about his brother Methodius too, as far as his personality was concerned. He was a fighter, just like his brother – a fighter for a cause, the Slavonic liturgy which had to be defended against its enemies, and he was at times driven to considerable anger and resentment against his enemies.

And Methodius had his enemies – the German missionaries were already working in Moravia and resented Eastern interference. The brothers went to Rome where Cyril died and Methodius was consecrated a bishop by the pope. More than a thousand years ahead of his time, Methodius secured papal approval for celebrating the liturgy in the vernacular. In theory this should have solved his problems but the German bishops set up a campaign of episcopal harassment, including the use of forged papal letters and unjustified imprisonment, to force Methodius out of Moravia.

Eventually Methodius took refuge in Bulgaria, a country which after some doubt had thrown in its lot with the Church of the East and with Photius, the patriarch of Constantinople. Nigel Wilson says that the king of Bulgaria, Boris I, was always flirting politically with the pope and he obviously wanted to play off one side against the other. In the end he must have decided that it was a good idea to be on satisfactory terms with his closest neighbour, Byzantium. Paganism had been very deeply entrenched in Bulgaria and so Boris wrote sometimes to Photius and sometimes to the pope with questions about the effect of adopting Christianity on the population at large. Questions like – could Christians have baths on Wednesdays and Fridays? Was it all right to have sex on Sundays? What about the wearing of trousers? The pope dismissed that question as unnecessary. But there were practical difficulties as well of a more serious kind. The Bulgarians wanted to know quite justifiably what you do if you have an army in the field which is committed to the practice of Christianity because obviously in the army you do certain things that are not in agreement with Christian precepts. The Byzantines managed to satisfy them somehow, but they had to send many missionaries out to convince them.

Methodius died in Bulgaria. In the end both the Church of the West and the Church of the East recognised the value of the brothers' untiring missionary work. Their accomplishment was not only religious but also literary as Sir Dimitri Obolensky explains. The language into which

Cyril, Methodius, and their collaborators translated the Byzantine texts was intelligible to the whole Slav world. This language, the Old Church Slavonic language, intelligible as it was to all the Slavs, was in the course of time enriched by more translations of Byzantine religious and secular texts and by the composition of original works in that language. So this Old Church Slavonic, the creation of Cyril and Methodius, became after Greek and Latin the third international language of Europe.

When Boris of Bulgaria had been conducting his dual correspondence course in practical theology the pope of Rome was Nicholas and the patriarch of Constantinople Photius. Apart from being rivals for Boris's letters, the two men had been at loggerheads for some time. Photius, a cultured man of the world, had come to the patriarchate in an unconventional way. The emperor Michael's uncle, Bardas, left his wife and chose to live instead with his young daughter-in-law. He was roundly condemned by the ascetic patriarch Ignatius. The emperor intervened; Ignatius was deposed and Photius, although a layman at the time, was chosen as patriarch elect and swept through all the stages of ordination and consecration at breakneck speed. The pope took Ignatius' side. The patriarchate of Constantinople and the papacy of Rome had in theory a relationship of younger and older brother, and it was as fraught with tension as such a relationship often is.

Added to that the patriarchate and the papacy had evolved into very different institutions. Dr Herrin says that in contrast to the patriarch of Constantinople, who lived in the political capital of the empire and always remained very severely under imperial control, the pope, as bishop of Rome, had complete independence in the definition of dogma and theology, but absolutely no secular assistance in the imposing of that theology. So the patriarch of Constantinople could invoke the imperial armies against heretics, whereas in the West, if the bishop of Rome wished to impose correct Christian faith on, for example, the Lombards who had settled in northern Italy and kept threatening Rome, he had no secular forces apart from a small Byzantine garrison and a few men-at-arms whom he paid personally as his bodyguards. He had no secular army to send against heretics in the West and therefore his authority was of a very different nature. He represented St Peter and the continuity of the donation by Christ himself to St Peter as the Rock on which he would build his Church. The bishops of Rome clung to that authority which made them supreme in the West, but they had no capacity to impose their own definitions of Christianity.

Nicholas called on Photius to resign. The patriarch refused. Rome and Constantinople broke off relations – a brief schism until Ignatius was reinstated three years later. This is usually referred to as the Photian schism. An inaccurate term, Bishop Kallistos believes, because in the middle of the ninth century we should not speak of a schism. Christians in East and West still had the sense that they belonged to one Church. When Photius quarrelled with pope Nicholas most of their contemporaries did not feel that meant the two Churches were divided. What happened in the ninth century was that Photius brought into the open the main element that was going to cause problems later on – the addition in the West of the word *Filioque* to the Creed. The Creed in the West says that the Holy Spirit proceeds from the Father *and from the Son*. In the original version, preserved by the Orthodox unchanged, it says simply that the Holy Spirit proceeds from the Father. Photius thought that the Western addition was heresy, and accused the West of this. In his second patriarchate Photius was in communion with Rome, so there was no permanent schism, but the *Filioque* problem was not resolved and Photius did not withdraw his opinion that the West was heretical, so the seeds of later controversy were sown.

Photius was also a great literary figure. His main work the *Bibliotheca* contains the summaries of nearly 300 books, giving a unique opportunity for scholars to see into the mind of a ninth-century Greek. Some of the books mentioned are only known through Photius' summaries. His learning was considered so immense that a rumour started that his knowledge came as the result of a pact made with a Jewish magician. Photius' religious statements contain a hint of the troubles which would eventually result in the great schism of 1054.

Nigel Wilson says that Photius crystallised the differences between the Greek Church and the Roman Church. He made it clear that the claim of the pope to be the final arbiter in Church disputes was in question. On the more doctrinal side, he made it clear that the Greek Church would not accept the Roman position on *Filioque*. Once he had set out the Greek position on that issue and on the question of papal primacy, the lines of battle were drawn up, and the Greek Church in essence had defined its position, which it maintained through thick and thin in later centuries, greatly to the disadvantage of Byzantium and ultimately of Europe.

The dispute known as the *Filioque* clause still divides the Church of the East and the Church of the West. But it is important not to overstate it. Photius died in full communion with Rome although sticking to his theological guns. Neither Kasia nor Photius would have considered they lived in a Church divided in two. There is another story about Kasia, not drawn from her Byzantine debutante days but from her days as abbess.

Theophilus apparently had not been able to forget her. Years after their first meeting he came to her monastery. She saw him coming and fled. He burst into her cell and found a piece of paper on her desk with a half-written poem. The emperor completed the poem. An unlikely story. Emperors do not belong in abbeys. Abbesses do not belong in courts. But it is a useful story – a reminder of how court and church in Byzantium were inextricably linked.

In the years to come relations between the Church of the East and the Church of the West would be hobbled by complicity politics and in particular by the legacy of Charlemagne confirmed in ceremony at the beginning of the ninth century. Dr Herrin says that when, on Christmas Day 800, pope Leo III crowned Charles, king of the Franks, as Holy Roman emperor in Rome, he re-established the notion that there was an empire in the West and that the pope had given it a particular authority by crowning the reigning king as emperor. Subsequently Charlemagne reigned and imposed a Christian faith in the West with that authority. And as the ninth century passed by, the whole question of how the emperors of the West were to relate to those who regarded themselves as the emperors in the East, and the only representatives of the Roman authority that they had inherited from Constantine I, became more and more prominent. The relations between these two imperial powers added a very political factor in the separation of the Churches and time and again we find that it is because the emperors of East and West are in dispute that the Churches of Constantinople and of Rome come into conflict. From now on theological problems are also matters of court politics. Kasia was able to turn her back on the imperial court – a freedom which the Churches as a whole would find more and more impossible.

ANGELS VERSUS A GOD
OF THUNDER
.

While Kasia, the sharp-tongued abbess of Byzantium, was spending her old age writing her final poems and hymns, Photius the polymath, the civil servant turned patriarch, made an extraordinary claim. In a letter which survives to this day he boasts that even the fierce and bloodthirsty people of Rus had accepted baptism at the hands of Greek missionaries. The lands of the north were now Christian. That success seems to have been short-lived but the over-optimistic claim would eventually become a prophecy. Towards the end of the tenth century the people of Rus did indeed become Christian – not because of missionaries sent north by a patriarch but because of reports prepared by envoys sent south to Constantinople by a pagan prince.

> The prince's ambassadors gazed spellbound at the beauty of the Church of Hagia Sophia. Their eyes moved from the paintings of the saints and martyrs to the gold and silver of the altar. They stared at the richness of the priests' vestments. They drank in the smell of incense and were captured by the tide of the rising and falling chants. In their exaltation they could not tell whether they were on earth or in heaven. They readily believed that every day a chorus of angels descended from heaven to join in the services.

The prince to whom the envoys reported back was Vladimir of Kiev, a man with five wives, eight hundred concubines, a reputation for brutality, and a determined grandmother. And it is Vladimir's conversion which was marked in 1988 by the millennium celebrations of the Russian Orthodox Church. Vladimir, or Volodymyr, is rarely or skimpily mentioned in most history books. Yet his decision to become a Christian was beyond a doubt the most important step taken by any ruler in the tenth century. However mixed his motives, his baptism cast the mould of the culture not only of the Rus, the people of the Kiev kingdom, but also of the Russian empire and to a large extent of the Soviet people today. It is Vladimir who determined that Russia would feel it belonged to Europe, but more particularly to Eastern Europe. Blame Vladimir for the fact that the Soviet Union uses the Cyrillic alphabet and feels uneasy about the West.

The tenth century was not a period of glory for the West. There were few inspiring leaders and the papacy was in its most sordid decline,

VOLODIMIR I.

il monta sur le trône, en 981,

et regna 35. ans.

Vladimir, Prince of Kiev, who had 800 concubines, brought Christianity to the land of the Rus and invented meals-on-wheels

treading a monotonous path of scandal, muddle and murder. The court of Byzantium was hardly any better. One emperor dabbled in astrology, another became a byword for inertia. Imperial poisonings, intrigues and affaires took the place of politics. The power bases of East and West might be weary, but one group of people was ready for action – the Varangians – or – to put it in words which Dunstan, the tong-wielding archbishop of Canterbury, and Aethelred the Unready would understand – the Vikings were on the move.

The Vikings who had so harried England were part of a far larger movement of territorial expansion. They not only attacked England but they regularly crossed Europe by a trade route second only to the Silk Road – the Viking river route to Byzantium. They traded fur, honey, wax and slaves for wine, oil and silk, with the odd bit of pillaging thrown in. Their influence in the north from west to east was incalculable.

And Vladimir, prince of Kiev, was part of this expansion. He belonged to a ruling house which was more Scandinavian than Slav. His grandmother's name Olga was merely a Slav version of Helga. The name Vladimir itself comes from the Scandinavian Waldemar. Vladimir's people, the Rus, were a mixture of Swedish/Viking and Slav; an imposing but pagan people according to Ibn Fadlan, the traveller and diplomat, who journeyed west and north on the caliph of Baghdad's business. In his diary, Ibn Fadlan describes the Rus as tall as date palms, blond-haired, red-faced, strong and healthy. He also describes their pre-Christian religious practices and in particular gives harrowing eye-witness accounts of a funeral.

Dr Hilda Davidson says Ibn Fadlan had been told that the Rus had extraordinary funeral customs so he was delighted when he heard that one of the leaders had either been killed or died and they were having a funeral for him. He witnessed the whole funeral in great detail. His account is now famous. He describes in gruesome detail how one of the slave girls volunteered to die at the funeral. The leader who died must have been of royal birth or high birth, because such a fuss was made for him. He was given wonderful clothes to go to the next world in and elaborate preparations for the funeral were put in hand. Meanwhile he was buried as a temporary measure. They then dug him up for the great cremation ceremony. During the preparations the girl who had volunteered to die had been treated like a queen. Before the cremation ceremony she was heavily plied with drink, so it is possible that the full terror of her impending state was clouded. But the description of her being killed is harrowing. Finally she was burned on a ship together with her official husband. The idea was that she would be received into the next world as his wife. The most interesting part of the account is the ceremony in which she was lifted up by two men and looked over a gate and said she could see the other world. She could see all her kinsmen there and her husband who was calling for her to go to him.

As prince of the Rus, Vladimir ruled over an uncompromisingly pagan people. Kiev was a trading city renowned for its favoured position on the river Dnieper dominating the river route to Byzantium. The city was prosperous but it was *not* a centre of culture. There are no contemporary accounts of tenth-century Kiev because writing only came with the missionaries summoned by Vladimir. Any assessment of Vladimir's character before his baptism has to be drawn from the bare historical bones of his actions, not from reports of his words.

Dr John Roberts, Warden of Merton College, Oxford, says that we can draw a lot of conclusions from his behaviour. He was clearly a cunning, brave, fierce, and ingenious man. He would not have secured the diplomatic and strategic success he did if that had not been the case. He was also a man who was inured to violence. Two of his brothers had been killed on his own bloody way to the throne. His father had been killed in battle and his skull made into a drinking cup. It was a world of violence in which you had to have the virtues (if that is the word) of a violent man in order to succeed.

The same was true of women. Vladimir's grandmother, Olga, was made of stern stuff. After her husband Igor had been killed by the Drevlians who objected to his enthusiastic tax collection system, Olga invited the Drevlians' envoys to a banquet, waited until they were drunk, and then had them all murdered. To press the point home she then sent out soldiers who burned down their town and killed 5000 of them. Olga ruled as regent for her son Sviatoslav, Vladimir's father. In her old age she made a strange decision. At about the time of Vladimir's birth, she visited Byzantium and asked to be received into the Christian Church. As a trading partner and a convert she was received with open arms.

Dr Hilda Davidson says that Olga had a whole month in Byzantium, which is chronicled in great detail in the *Book of Ceremonies*. We know all the receptions that were held there, the places she went to, where she met the emperor and how much she was expected to behave. Ordinary people who went there had to prostrate themselves by going flat on the floor three times before the emperor, while he on his automated throne shot up like a cinema organ. But Olga did not have to do this. We are told that she simply nodded politely and gave a little bow. This was a great honour, it meant that she was recognised as a ruler, which was fair enough.

Olga (right), Vladimir's strong-minded grandmother who went to Byzantium in search of baptism despite her son Sviatoslav's disapproval

Sviatoslav her son was usually away fighting and she looked after his children, her grandchildren, and so she was really the regent of Kiev in more than name and was honoured in her own right as a ruler. When she returned from Byzantium her son said he had no intention of being a Christian. 'My bodyguard would laugh at me,' he said.

Vladimir's father may have been dismissive of Olga's new-found religion, but children do not learn from their fathers alone. Metropolitan Anthony, leader of the Russian Orthodox Church in Great Britain and Ireland, believes that the key to understanding Vladimir's ultimate conversion can be found in the babushkas of twentieth-century Russia. Vladimir's father was a passionate pagan who considered Christianity a religion for slaves – a weak religion for weak people. He was a warlike warlord and so Vladimir was brought up in a court that despised Christianity. But he was under the influence of a grandmother who had proved able to stand alone, like so many women in Russia were able to stand alone in the times of the darkest persecutions and had saved the Church. She had proved capable of standing alone, keeping her faith, never being ashamed of it, in spite of the mockeries that surrounded it, and gave to Vladimir a sense that there is another dimension to things.

But Professor Ihor Ševčenko, of Harvard University, thinks there may be another reason why Vladimir found a religion fit for slaves attractive. Vladimir himself was an illegitimate son of Sviatoslav, and that is perhaps of some importance in reconstructing his decision to join the world of Christianity. He was the son of a servant of his grandmother, and he had some trouble with this because one of the princesses to whom he proposed marriage said, according to the *Chronicle*, that she would not take the boots off the feet of the son of a slave. Whereupon he conquered the city and forced her to marry him.

From his earliest days as ruler Vladimir was fully aware of the power of religion as a unifying force. At first he tried to organise the confusion of Turcic, Slav, Finno-Ugrian and Scandinavian gods and godlets and local cults into one pantheon headed by Peroun, the thunder god, whose distinctive statues always had wooden bodies, silver heads and gold moustaches. But this new organised paganism brought with it few advantages. It was not particularly popular at home and opened up no new trade routes and made him no new foreign friends.

So his next consideration, according to Dr Sergei Hackel, Vicar General of the Russian Orthodox Church in Great Britain, was, as far as we can tell from the chronicles of a later date, to see which of the world religions might be that much more suitable. How he came across these world religions we cannot be sure, but the later chronicles tell us that emissaries came from them. They came from Islam – which was the neighbouring religion. They came from Judaism. They came from Western Christendom, and they came from the Byzantine empire, from what we would now call the Orthodox Christian part of the world. He listened to them all with interest. He cross-examined them, and in due course he sent out emissaries of his own to the various parts of the world from which those earlier visitors had come. Judaism did not interest him by that time. He was rather put off by the fact that Judaism was a religion of exiles. They had been defeated, so he thought that perhaps their God was not up to much. But he did send emissaries to the Western Christian world and to the Eastern Christian world, and to Islam. The *Chronicle* says rather wryly that Islam in due course was not to appeal to the emissaries any more than it was to Vladimir. When he heard of the prohibition of alcohol that was normal in Islam, he uttered the well-remembered words, 'We cannot do without it,' a lesson Mr Gorbachev was to learn a thousand years later.

So Islam was ruled out. Western Christianity seemed too dry and too lack-lustre. Byzantium put on a better show. The emperor Basil II told the patriarch to pull out all the liturgical stops for Vladimir's representatives. Little wonder they could not tell whether the worship in Hagia Sophia belonged to this world or the next. For all their reputation for savagery, the hearts of the Rus were captivated once and for all by the sheer beauty of Eastern Orthodox worship.

But apart from liturgy there was a political side to the Rus conversion. As Dr John Roberts says, Byzantium needed Vladimir. It needed Vladimir because Vladimir presided over the country which still provided fighting men who could help Byzantium. After all, what if Kiev became Romanised? What if it fell into the hands of a Roman Church like the Poles or the Moravians? If that happened another potential rival would have established itself across the trade routes of the southern Russian rivers and there might be even worse troubles stored up in the future, because that rival would be able to call upon allies in the West. It was very much in the interest of Byzantium that Kiev was Christianised from Constantinople.

Indeed Basil was so keen to have Vladimir as an ally that he made an unprecedented offer. If Vladimir would help the Byzantines in the field, he could have Anna, the emperor's sister, in marriage. The political advantages of such an alliance are obvious. But what about faith? Was Vladimir a *believing* Christian? It depends what is meant by belief, says Dr Simon Franklin, Fellow of Clare College, Cambridge. If belief is something which obviously works, is efficacious, then Vladimir believed in Christianity. If it means belief in the correct Trinitarian doctrines – that would be difficult to say. On theological matters, early Russian writing is peculiarly slap-dash. Even the Creed which Vladimir supposedly adopted, as written down in the chronicle about Vladimir's conversion, is actually heretical on the nature of the Trinity. This is not because the Russians were heretics but because the Greeks who were giving them their religion, their books, and material to translate, said, 'Here is an old Creed – take that.' And they did not bother to look. Translators translated mechanically and shoved it in, not being particularly interested in the fineries of Trinitarian disputes. Depth of commitment is difficult to assess, but Vladimir was undoubtedly impressed by Christianity.

Whatever the political machinations there can be no doubt that Vladimir returned from his baptism and marriage in the Crimean city of Cherson, with a convert's zeal for making new converts. As Dr Sergei Hackel says, having come home as a Christian, his intention was to have not only his élite but the people in general converted to the Christian faith. He sent out an edict to the people telling them to assemble on a certain day by the River Dnieper, where they would be baptised. Those who did not assemble for baptism would incur his displeasure. We must presume that his displeasure would not have been very pleasant to encounter and we must also presume that the majority of the population followed his orders and came down to that river and that a mass baptism of the people took place. According to the Russian chronicle, people of all ages thanked God, very full of joy. But there must also have been a great deal of violation of people's consciences. The fact that it was not necessarily as peaceful as all that is shown by a phrase which survived in a now lost chronicle which speaks of two of Vladimir's lieutenants, Putsiata and Dobrynia, who went out into the northern parts of the Kievan realm, to Novgorod, where Putsiata baptised with the sword and Dobrynia with fire.

Not only had southern ways of worship come north, northern military strength had found an unlikely home in the south. Vladimir's men who joined the imperial Varangian or Viking bodyguards in Constantinople found themselves in an odd position of trust. They, the outsiders, were trusted with the keys of the imperial treasury. This may seem hard to believe from a twentieth-century Western view of pillaging Scandinavians, but other transformations were afoot as well – notably in the behaviour of Vladimir himself.

Metropolitan Anthony says that certain things changed radically. First, his morals changed radically. He became a Christian in his personal behaviour, but also he introduced into Kiev something which we could call social Christianity. For instance, we know for sure that he abolished the death penalty. He said he had no right to take the life of anyone to whom God has given life. And he had to be preached at by his Byzantine converters to say that there are cases when this is a necessity. He opened his court daily to the hungry. Every day they could all come and eat at his palace, not in his own banqueting room, but in the court. Those people who were too old, or too infirm to come, received food that was taken round the city in carts, the first meals-on-wheels. So a real concrete Christian action emerged out of his conversion.

Even in architectural terms Vladimir's conversion formed the mould of Russian cities for centuries to come. As Dr Simon Franklin says, there were no monumental stone buildings in Kiev before Vladimir built his large tithe church. The building of monuments, the physical presence of Christianity, changed the landscape of the cities, and in that respect Vladimir and his successors ensured that Christianity was a focus, not just of spiritual life, but of urban planning.

Vladimir's legacy is controversial. Who are the descendants of his people, the Rus? The Russians? The Ukrainians? Dr Sergei Hackel thinks it is very misleading to introduce modern terminology such as Russian, let alone Ukrainian. In 1988 there was quite a dispute about whose Millennium it was, the Millennium of the baptisms of the Rus, the Ukrainians or the Russians. The Ukrainians claim it as theirs, because Kiev nowadays is in the Ukraine. Russians have nothing to do with it, they say. But Rus does not mean any of the things which we would now like it to mean. There were various tribes, various ethnic groups, which we would not recognise as either Russian, Ukrainian or even Slav. And the ruling dynasty is by origin a Scandinavian dynasty, and Vladimir had personal links with the Scandinavian world.

In the western edge of Europe that Scandinavian world was synonymous with terror and wanton destruction. Dunstan of Glastonbury, the great tenth-century English saint and monastic reformer, would have known only of Vikings as the plague barely healed by the efforts of Alfred the Great. Vladimir the prince and Dunstan the monk, who is credited with having pinched the devil's nose with a pair of tongs, had one thing in common – the belief that Christianity had inevitable social and political implications.

The Reverend Douglas Dales, Chaplain and Head of Religious Studies at Marlborough College, Wiltshire, says that Dunstan brought deep theological convictions about Christian leadership to bear upon how politics should be conducted. His legislation bears a lot of Christian influence, in the handling of prisoners, and the setting up of a standard coinage, standard weights and measures, so that the poor would not be robbed. He was a man who was not only an archbishop and legislator and a very effective administrator and diplomat, a good leader of bishops, an abbot, a tremendous influence over young people, a very great educator,

This tenth-century Christ is believed to be by Dunstan. The figure beneath the inscription, 'Christ, I pray, protect me Dunstan', is thought to be a self-portrait

but also a scholar. We have documents which he corrected and edited and he went on doing this right through life, even when he was an old man at Canterbury. He was also a musician, an artist, a metal worker, a craftsman of very great skills – a man who could turn his hand to making organs and bells for monasteries and who could draw wonderful pictures. We only have one left, the famous picture of Christ with Dunstan at his feet. He was a man who had an amazing musical gift and one of his plain-chants is still sung on his day. He received it while he was asleep in visions from heaven. There was a charismatic dimension to this extraordinary musical creativity which persisted right to the end of his life.

But Dunstan, the embroiderer and composer, was an almost solitary if versatile light on the western Christian horizon. As Dr John Roberts says, when Vladimir was on the throne in Kiev, his opposite number in England was Aethelred the Unready, and he was just beginning to have to cope with a new wave of Scandinavian attacks from the family relations of Vladimir on his shores. Kiev was in some ways a richer, more splendid city than much of the West could show at that time. If you were looking for splendour, urban splendour, civilised splendour in the tenth century, you did not look for it in France, or in England, or even in Ottonian Germany, and certainly not amid the ruins of Rome. You looked for it in Constantinople, Baghdad, perhaps in Cordoba, or Seville and the Arab cities, and you could see the beginnings of it in Kiev.

In Kiev, Vladimir was presiding over the birth of a new order. He and Olga are revered as the firstborn of Russian Orthodox saints. Their stories have been told and retold, each time with a new layer of folklore, but even the hagiographers have never attempted to portray Vladimir as being whiter than white. Dr Simon Franklin thinks he knows why. Vladimir is said to have had countless wives and even more countless concubines and the subject of fornication crops up in the account of his life before his conversion with a frequency which is embarrassing for hagiographers. It is the main element in the description of his character which we get in the primary chronicle. But we have to regard the tales with scepticism, because we have to take into account the motives of the people who were writing them. The people who were writing about Vladimir were not trying to create a picture of a promiscuous and violent ruler, they were trying to create a picture of a ruler as saint – so why do they dwell on his promiscuity? Not because of their historiographical conscience that they had to record the truth, whatever it might contain, however embarrassing it might be, but because the blacker his character is before his conversion, the greater, the more majestic the miracle of the fact that he became Christian. He was like the rest of us, only more so – even greater in his vices, therefore even greater in his virtues.

Whatever the debates about Vladimir's motives, the majesty of the Christian legacy he gave to his people and their descendants can be in no doubt. In the years following the Millennium of his baptism, is the Russian Orthodox church in any way recognisable as the child of his faith? Metropolitan Anthony thinks it is – although he says it is not always easy to recognise an oak from an acorn. Vladimir was a warrior, but what he had seen in Olga and also in himself made him feel that the pagan gods and paganism as such were too poor to fill his soul. What he saw were the beginnings. What developed later was something infinitely complex because it was not only a faith in the Church, it was a whole culture. There was no Russian culture before him. But Metropolitan Anthony heard the late Andrei Gromyko speak on the role of the Church and Gromyko said that it was the Church which had given a shape to Russian culture, the Church which had made it possible for Russian statesmanship to develop, the Church which was the power that united all the Russian principalities into a vast empire, and gave a morality to the country. Vladimir the prince who became a saint remains one of the greatest lasting influences on a state which officially does not share his faith and on his many spiritual descendants who do.

'THE DREAM OF JERUSALEM'

.

More than one hundred years after Vladimir, prince of Kiev, sinner and saint, had ordered his people to accept baptism in the river Dnieper, a tall, severe, bearded Frenchman made an open-air speech so impassioned that it launched an extravagant dream of chivalry which would revolutionise Christendom and would grip Europe for centuries to come in convulsions of glory and shame.

> *I beg you and plead with you. Go to Jerusalem, the centre of the world, an earthly heaven, the jewel of that holy land which has been made for ever sacred by our Saviour who lived, suffered, died and was buried there. Jerusalem the city of the King of Kings is now held prisoner by our godless enemies. Jerusalem weeps and is humiliated. She is forced to take part in infidel rituals. She longs to be free. Go to her aid. Free the burial place of Our Lord. Seize back the land taken by pagans.*
>
> *Do not be afraid.*
>
> *Those who die on that journey will have their sins immediately forgiven. I pledge this by the power God has vested in me.*

The speaker was Odo de Lagery, better remembered as Urban II, the pope who lit the fuse of the First Crusade. Many bigotries and theological nonsenses look to him as founding father. Nevertheless Odo was far from a fanatic. He was monkish, well organised and at times disastrously misunderstood. From his youth Odo had been a high-flier. He came from Châtillon-sur-Marne in nothern France. His family belonged to the minor nobility there. As a young man Odo had become a canon at Rheims Cathedral. From there he had moved to the greatest abbey of his day, Cluny, where he rose to become prior. Before long he was talent-spotted by the cardinal bishop of Ostia and was summoned to assist Gregory VII, the great reforming pope. Odo quickly climbed the Church's bureaucratic ladder. In 1088 he was elected pope and Odo became Urban. The task which confronted him was not an easy one. The Church of the East and the Church of the West were in schism and closer to home there were the constant problems of politicking, plotting and anti-popes. Papal survival was an achievement in itself. But Urban, the former monk, proved stronger than many expected.

et aultres sains lieux la enuiron. enduites. Et comment Il
Et les ypiens ylhabitans z demou les tenoient en trop oprobzieuse
rans. z que les aultres par eulx captiuite z seruage. ou nestoyent
tyranniquement z Inhumaine deshonneur z oprobze de tous
ment tues. Ils auoient referue les ypiens. Conduuant z mou
en Infructueuse vie a fin que sur strant par duerses raisons tres
eulx en soprobze du saint nom euidentes que le saint peuple
ypien puissent continuer plus ypien ne debuoit plus souffir
souuement leurs Insatiables nendurer que ses sains lieux et

Odo de Lagery, better known as pope Urban II, causes a mortgage boom by calling on the Christian knights of Europe to go on crusade and free the Holy Land

The Reverend John Cowdrey, Senior Research Fellow in Modern History at St Edmund Hall, Oxford, says that Urban II was a very measured and cautious man, a man of great prudence, a very cool man in many ways, but he also had a great charisma of his own. He had an unfailing talent for dealing with other people – getting them to behave in ways that he wanted, getting them round to his point of view, very often claiming them back from loyalty to the anti-pope – just the man to restore the fortunes of the papacy so that it had durability for the rest of the central Middle Ages.

Urban's century, the eleventh, was an extraordinary period in Christian history. It was a time of tremendous energy, unquestionable heroism, material sacrifice, some thuggery, and not a little madness. In the West, after the doldrums of the tenth century, there was a new spirit of reconstruction and religious reform. In the East it was a time of panic. The Seljuk Turks battered Byzantium's authority and took half its empire. Worse was to follow. Jerusalem, the city revered throughout the Christian world as a living testimony to the Incarnation, was captured by the Turks. Christians of East and West separated by formal schism in 1054 found common cause against the Saracens about whose faith they knew nothing.

The eleventh century became a rich breeding ground for anti-Semitism, idealism and hysteria. And the weather did not help. Urban preached the First Crusade against a background of meteorological phenomena which must have been terrifying to live through. There were meteor showers, two eclipses of the moon and one of the sun. The sky turned red on more than one occasion. Added to that there were epidemics of ergotism or holy fire, a sickness caused by eating fungus-ridden rye bread. Eccentrics and visionaries abounded. Peter the Hermit, who would eat only fish and drink only wine, claimed he had been sent a letter from Heaven. The crusading count Emich of Leiningen, together with his murderous anti-Semitic followers, revered a goat and a goose – both they believed were full of the Holy Spirit.

There were voices of moderation too. Anselm of Canterbury, a supporter of Urban, warned that the earthly Jerusalem must never be seen as more important than the heavenly one. But in the minds of the faithful the two were hopelessly intertwined. Above all there was a feeling of intense religious revivalism and holy terror. Professor Jonathan Riley-Smith, Head of the Department of History at the Royal Holloway and Bedford New College, University of London, says that the churches embarked on a very intense programme of evangelisation. The leaders of the reform were mostly monks. The morality that they were putting forward to the laity was a monastic morality. And they were demanding of the laity a standard of morality which was far far beyond anything they could hope to reach.

There is a very famous vision of purgatory. A south Italian monk dreamt he was being taken through purgatory when he came upon a ladder with red-hot rungs, with its feet in a basin of boiling pitch. Men were scrambling up and down this ladder howling in agony, down into the pitch and up again. These men were not blasphemers, heretics, fornicators; they were married men who had slept with their wives on the forbidden days which were Wednesdays, Fridays and Sundays, certain of the Feast Days, all of Lent, all of Advent, a period of penitence before 14 September, several weeks before and several weeks after the birth of a baby. What layman could hope to come up to such standards? But Professor Riley-Smith says the fascinating thing about the eleventh-century laity, unlike us who when faced with the Church making great demands on us tend to give it the two fingers, is that they worried terribly and felt immense guilt. They were very conscious of their own sinfulness, a sinfulness from which they could never escape. This preoccupation can be seen in charters to religious houses, in which they describe their hopes and anxieties for the future – the keynote is fear of eternal damnation.

The standards of religious and moral behaviour which ordinary Christians felt they should live by might seem impossibly high but there was another more down-to-earth side to faith. Right across Europe there was a frenzy of church building. Every village, no matter how poor, had its church. There, not only would Mass be said and psalms sung, but also beer would be brewed, plays performed, and markets held. Literally and physically the church held community life together. Religion could not be separated from daily life. You behaved in church as you would outside – even during the services.

According to Professor Gordon Davies, the forms of devotion in those days were very different from what obtains in western Europe at the present day. They were more like present-day Eastern Orthodox worship. If you wanted to get up and go outside, you got up and went outside. If you wanted to talk to somebody, you went across and talked. Whereas, because of the Protestant Reformation, we tend to be drilled, stuck fast in an auditorium, never moving, listening to words and more words. The whole thing is very solemn. If any child raises its voice, 'Tut tut tut', that is not the right thing. That was not the atmosphere of worship in the Middle Ages.

'*Et in Spiritum Sanctum Dominum et vivificantem qui ex Patre Filioque procedit.*' 'I believe in the Holy Spirit, lord and life-giver who proceeds from the Father and the Son.' Those words which, no matter how similar the atmosphere of Eastern and Western Christian worship, drove a wedge between the two Churches. The problem was not new. It was the cause of the rift between patriarch Photius and pope Nicholas in the ninth century. The grounds for argument remained the same. The Church of the West had added one word '*Filioque*', meaning 'and from the Son', to the Creed. So in the West a Christian said the Holy Spirit proceeded from the Father *and* the Son. The dispute was old. It had first cropped up in Spain in the sixth century as part of a campaign to stress the divinity of Christ. In the East they kept the form of the Holy Spirit proceeding from the Father alone. In Constantinople the *Filioque* clause was proof of papal high-handedness and also bad theology. To modern ears it all sounds like a storm in a wine cup.

Was it inevitable that the one word would split Christendom? Dr Judith Herrin believes that even in the 1050s it would have been possible

Peter the Hermit, who would eat only fish and drink only wine, leading his crusaders

to salvage the estrangement and prevent the schism of 1054. In 1024 the emperor Basil II had sent an embassy to Rome to try and patch up differences, to try and recognise that different customs had developed over the centuries. It was felt that the questions of whether priests should be married, whether they should shave, when they should fast, whether they should have leavened or unleavened bread, whether they should add water to the wine for the sacrament could be sorted out. The theological question of the procession of the Holy Ghost really was a problem and it might have proved a stumbling block, but with good will the schism that came about in 1054 might have been prevented. The good will was lacking, firstly because pope Leo IX died and the cardinal, Humbert of Silva Candida, was a very forthright man who wished to negotiate for the papacy before the next pope was elected. He wished to take that authority upon himself and to insist upon Roman customs. Secondly, the good will was lacking because the patriarch, Michael Cerularius, was a very forceful man who had been appointed to head the Church of Constantinople by a rather weak emperor.

Pope and patriarch excommunicated one another. It was a contest which no one won. By the time Urban came to the papacy the problem had festered for thirty years. He lifted the excommunication ban on the emperor in Byzantium and called a council at Bari to unknot the *Filioque* tangle. No solution was forthcoming and the Churches are still divided. But Sir Dimitri Obolensky maintains that it is important not to get things out of proportion. 'The Great Schism' is an unhelpful and inaccurate title, he says. The events of 1054 should be seen as a particularly dramatic moment in a very long process which combined mutual alienation, and mutual contact, between the two Churches of the East and West. We know that after 1054 the two Churches still had contacts with each other and a consciousness that Christendom was still a single body. A united whole survived this episode of 1054. Those mutual excommunications between the papal legates and the patriarch of Constantinople, which did not involve their respective Churches, were only personal excommunications, and for a long time afterwards, well into the thirteenth century or even beyond, there is plenty of evidence in certain parts of Europe, particularly in the Balkans, of a consciousness of a still united Christendom.

Healing the Great Schism or the not-all-that-great mutual alienation was one of Urban's major preoccupations. It was undoubtedly an important element of what made him decide to declare a crusade. He seems, says the Reverend John Cowdrey, to have been very anxious at the beginning to try to do something to restore the broken unity between the Eastern and the Western parts of Christendom – between Rome and Constantinople. And he seems to have seen the significance of a crusade as a focus for any attempt to do that. He was also very disturbed by the state of Western Europe with its feuds, its violence and its internal warfare, and he was determined to try and find some new outlet for the chivalry of Europe.

Urban decided to call on the Christian knights of Western Europe to take up arms on behalf of the Christians of the East. He saw the crusade as a military penitential pilgrimage in which soldiers would be soldiers of Christ not of any earthly general. The spoils of war would not be booty but grace. It was a complicated and heady idea. Urban decided to preach it first of all on home ground, with no holds barred.

From the late summer of 1095 to the late summer of 1096, pope Urban toured southern, central and western France, and according to Professor Riley-Smith there were extraordinary factors behind his trip. First of all Urban was a man of sixty, naturally reserved but the way he behaved could not be more theatrical. The great moment for the preaching of the First Crusade came within a month or two of his arrival in France. At Claremont on 27 November 1095, he preached the crusade in an open field outside the town. Claremont in November is very cold. But a dais was constructed in a field and pope Urban preached outside to a crowd – largely ecclesiastics and a few local notables – but it was great theatre.

We have eye-witness accounts of pope Urban's entry into certain towns – Limoges, for instance, and Tours. He was accompanied by an enormous flock of cardinals, archbishops and bishops from all over France, every one of them with his own entourage. This great assembly swept into these little country towns, and then pope Urban dedicated churches and was solemnly crowned. France in the late eleventh century was fragmented. The part under the king's control was confined to an area around Paris. Here was the pope with an enormous entourage entering towns and processing with crowds through streets which had never seen a king. Something of the excitement in the atmosphere is conveyed in the accounts. The nobles from the district collected together and they heard the pope preach. Judging from the words that have survived from his sermons, they were very carefully chosen to put maximum pressure on the nobility. Urban himself was the son of a petty lord from Champagne, so he knew exactly the audience he was addressing. He came from this class himself, so he knew just which buttons to press.

In calling the knights of Western Europe to go on crusade, Urban knew he was making no small demand. Financially, crusading was disastrous. Family land was mortgaged right, left and centre. To take your cross and go on crusade was to embark on the most expensive pilgrimage ever dreamt of. On the home front there was the danger of bankruptcy and of farms going to ruin. And greater horrors awaited the crusaders themselves.

As Professor Riley-Smith says, in 1096 large bodies of men and women left Western Europe with no system of supplies. There was no way in which those people could be provisioned. Once they crossed over to Asia Minor they passed even beyond Christian territory. They marched more than two thousand miles with no back-up whatever into unknown land with the intention of taking Jerusalem. It was an incredible venture and it is wrong to imagine that they were not conscious of the problems that would lie ahead. They were not unaware of what they were going into or unconscious of the problems or of the expense that they were undertaking. At the same time if you send 50,000 people out into Asia with no system of provisioning, the only way they are going to keep themselves alive is by foraging, and foraging leads to hooliganism. But they had no choice. It was that or perish.

The crusaders did not ride, they walked. The First Crusade lasted for three years and within eighteen months all the horses were dead. The crusade was not won by knights in shining armour charging the host of Asia, it was won by trudging on foot. Some crusaders ended up riding oxen. All of them faced the threat of disease. Given all that, what made these military pilgrims want to go on crusade?

Professor Gordon Davies says the crusaders had one motive which was not shared by other pilgrims. They were, as a contemporary account of the First Crusade says, out to avenge the honour of the outraged Jesus. In other words, they regarded Jesus as having suffered dishonour because infidels had taken over his place of burial and so they were out to avenge his honour. But they shared with all other pilgrims similar motives as well. All pilgrims went either to a local centre or to Jerusalem to obtain forgiveness. Indulgences were offered by the Church authorities, that is to say remission of penalties to be paid for sins committed. Both Urban II in 1095 and Eugene III in 1147 declared that everybody who took part in the crusades would receive absolution. The pilgrims also regarded their pilgrimage as a taking up of the Cross. They believed you could acquire holiness by going to a place which was regarded as an intersection point between everyday life and the life of God. The holiness was almost tangible, you could almost rub it off on yourself. And then they wanted to obtain relics. Robert II of Flanders, for example, was nicknamed by the Turks the Arm of St George because he managed to get hold of this arm when passing on the way to Palestine and was very devoted to it.

However elevated the crusaders' motives, they all knew they were engaged in a campaign which would involve bloodshed and murder. How was that reconciled with turning the other cheek? Professor Riley-Smith says that the stress throughout was that crusading is loving because you are expressing love of Christ, but never love of the enemy. The faithful would not have been able to comprehend that. Those who were transmitting the theology to the faithful sieved it. They sold the theology of charitable violence in terms the faithful would understand, that is in terms that were comprehensible to the member of a family whose brother or father might be oppressed or injured, or the member of a feudal nexus whose lord might be so injured. As soon as they did that the faithful responded in terms which they were used to, and that is with a vendetta, because their understanding of the response to one's brother or father being injured was to launch a blood feud. This comes across very clearly. One of the monastic commentators on the First Crusade produced, as part of his account, a sermon which he says was preached under the walls of Jerusalem. It never was, the words he quotes are his own but they are revealing. The sermon is nothing less than a call to a vendetta. 'What would you do if one of your blood relations was injured?' he asks. 'You know what you would do? Here you see your father, your brother oppressed, crucified.' This enabled the Church to rouse the laity even though it was very expensive and unpleasant for them. But the whole venture got out of hand, because once the preachers had taken the cork out of the bottle, they could not put it back again.

It would be wrong, however, to see Urban's century as a period of conveniently militarised theology. Anselm of Canterbury, mentioned by Dante as one of the spirits of light in the sphere of the sun, worked under Urban's aegis. While the First Crusade was in its early stages, Anselm had come to Rome to work on his bestselling *Cur Deus Homo* (Why God became Man). Anselm who was always at loggerheads with the kings of England had tackled the untackleable – the philosophical proof of God.

According to Dr Gillian Evans, Fellow in History at Fitzwilliam College, Cambridge, he says that it is possible to think of the greatest being you can imagine. It is also possible to think that such a supremely great being exists, as well as being a thought in your mind. And once you have thought that that being might exist, the thought that it might exist is actually greater than the thought that it is simply a thought. So to say that it is only a thought is not to think of the greatest thing that you can think of. So what we have now in front of our mind's eye is a being who is unimaginably great – the greatest we can think of and who also exists. That is the point at which Bertrand Russell and others have walked into lampposts, trying to see where Anselm has gone to – because he now says that, if we can think that thought, then God must exist in that reality which we have thought of him as existing in. Anselm's jump from what is in your head to what is in reality remains controversial.

St Anselm of Canterbury – a civilised man in need of a shave, he was loyal to Urban II and wrote theological bestsellers as well as campaigning against slavery

The intellectual life of the West was about to receive an unexpected stimulus. In the long run Urban's crusade would bring the West into contact with more than Saracen swords. Mashuq Ally says that one dimension that must not be missed is that, though there may have been two powers contending with each other, beneath that there was also the inter-cultural and intellectual exchange which was going on. Both contending powers brought with them scholarship, and people of piety. These people met each other and though wars were going on, there was a great, inter-cultural, inter-faith, intellectual exercise going on too. The

Muslims, having come to Europe, provided a springboard for what we today call Western civilisation.

Urban's crusade would indeed have many unforeseen consequences. The emperor of the East, Alexius Comnenus, had expected Urban to send him some crack mercenaries. He was not expecting 50,000 hungry and travel-weary volunteers who did not share one language let alone one commander. Anna, Alexius' daughter, described the crusaders who reached Byzantium in 1096.

> *They were all alight with holy zeal. Their faces were joyful and full of enthusiasm. Our streets were full. There were some Irish soldiers and behind them hundreds of ordinary people, men, women and children. All wearing the Red Cross on their shoulders.*

The motley crusaders were well treated in Byzantium. But the crusade was gaining a momentum of its own. The crusaders received co-operation from the Byzantine emperor, but the Reverend John Cowdrey thinks the crusade was something much bigger than Urban himself had thought he was going to stimulate, or Alexius Comnenus wanted when he addressed the papacy in 1095 for some kind of help. It became unwieldy and grew far beyond Urban's intentions for Byzantium.

Urban's call to crusade had another unwanted and unforeseen consequence. Anti semitism spread through Europe and Professor Riley-Smith believes Urban must have known about this but was powerless to stop it. Within months of his preaching the crusades, an appalling persecution of Jews, particularly in the Rhineland but also in France, had broken out. What the persecutors of the Jews were saying, and this is reported in Christian and in Hebrew sources, is that we have been called upon to avenge Christ, whose patrimony, Jerusalem, has been taken by the Muslims. But here, among us, are people who crucified Christ. How is it that we are called upon to march thousands of miles to avenge an injury to Christ, when among us are people who injured Christ – who disparaged his honour, as they put it, even more by crucifying him. The Church replied that it did not matter what happened in AD 33 or what happened in 634 when Jerusalem was taken by the Muslims – that was not the point. The point was what was happening there and then. The Jews were not injuring Christians at that time – they were totally harmless. The Muslims were not so harmless because they were occupying Christian lands. But it was too late. There is no written evidence of Urban's reaction to this, but he must have heard of it – and it would have appalled him.

Urban had other problems as well. Throughout his papacy his life was dogged by the anti-pope Clement III, a protégé of emperor Henry IV of Germany. This was not an isolated problem. It was a power struggle

The Eastern Emperor Alexius Comnenus who had expected a few highly trained mercenaries from Urban II – not 50,000 travel-weary volunteers

between Church and State, one which is well illustrated by Anselm of Canterbury's stormy relationship with the English royal house. Gillian Evans does not think the English monarchy had the slightest idea of what it was taking on in Anselm, because his reputation up to this point had been entirely as a holy and a learned man. He had shown no signs of being trouble at all, but once he became archbishop, being Anselm, he took his responsibility seriously and he took his duty to God and the king, in that order, equally seriously. Anselm had already given his allegiance to pope Urban II while he was at Bec. He could not in all conscience conceive of anybody else being pope, and that did not happen to suit the king. Connected with that was what we now call the Investiture Contest, which was a battle for supremacy between the authority of the State and the authority of the Church. The kings and emperors of Europe had fallen into the habit not only of selecting the person who was to be appointed to a bishopric or an archbishopric, but of investing that person with what were called 'the spiritualities of the see' – the ring and the star which symbolised the spiritual office. In doing that they were clearly going beyond their rights and powers. So it was a power struggle and Anselm was quite inadvertently caught up in it.

That power struggle between Church and State continues in many countries today. But it is not what Urban will be remembered for. In 1099 while he lay dying, Jerusalem was won. The end of the first and most successful crusade was celebrated in a frenzy of prayer, pillaging and unholy bloodlust. Urban died before the news reached Rome. Like most victories it was a mixed blessing, but one into which Professor Riley-Smith believes this generation should have an unprecedented insight.

The last twenty or thirty years have transformed crusade studies, he says. In the late eighteenth and nineteenth centuries, historians found the idea of holy war quite incomprehensible. So, unable to believe that individuals could be motivated by ideals, they looked for colonialism, or desire for material gain, or they simply said they were really just a load of marauding louts who did not really understand what they were doing. But we now live in an age in which there is militant Christian liberation, in which Christian violence has returned to the scene and is justified, theologically, in terms which are very similar to crusade propaganda. The crusades and the dream of Jerusalem should therefore be easier for us to understand.

THE SIBYL OF THE RHINE

•

A little more than forty years after Urban the eloquent had died in Rome without knowing that his dream of a Christian-controlled Jerusalem had become a reality, a highly-gifted middle-aged German woman who was small in stature, did not like cats, was unafraid of popes or of emperors, and is acclaimed by some as the unsung prophetess of the twentieth century, had a vision.

> *In the year of Our Lord 1141, when I was forty-two and seven months, I saw a mass of fiery light of the greatest brightness pouring down from the heavens. It enveloped my brain and my heart was kindled with a flame that did not burn me but warmed me as the sun warms the earth.*
>
> *From that moment on I knew and understood the meaning of the Psalms and the Gospels – as well as the other books of the Old and New Testaments. By 'understood' I do not mean that I was suddenly expert in evaluating the text, dividing the syllables and working out the cases and tenses. No, I understood the meaning.*

The visionary was Hildegard of Bingen – musician, ecologist, dramatist, apothecary, herbalist, cosmologist, preacher and prophetess. The fireball vision was by no means her first vision but it was a turning point in her life. It dispelled her doubts and gave her the courage to write and teach with a verve and a conviction which would make many uncomfortable.

Hildegard has always been controversial. In her own time, she was accused of hysteria and fraud. She organised the first-ever monastic strike. Nowadays she is hailed by some as the first female voice questioning the patriarchy of the Church. Others point to her statement that all science is of God as either an example of medieval naivety or as an insight which the scientific world is slowly coming to terms with.

Hildegard's life spanned most of the twelfth century. She was born in 1098 and died eighty years later. The youngest of ten children, at the age of eight, four years after the first of her visions, she was given as a living tithe to the anchoress Jutta who lived in a cell attached to the local Benedictine monastery of St Disibode. From there Hildegard watched the drama of the twelfth century unfold. It was a time of intellectual passion,

Man at the centre of the universe, painted either by Hildegard or under her direction, with a portrait of Hildegard in the bottom left-hand corner

old mysteries and new heresies, of sophistication and rank violence. Schoolmen, poets and lovers, Templars, Cathars and horse-breeding monks all contributed to the ferment which produced a unique renaissance of religious art and thought. It was the age of Thomas à Becket the martyr, of Barbarossa the tyrant, of Saladin the magnanimous infidel, and of the tragic Abelard and his Eloise.

Above all it was a period of immense artistic creativity, and one in which, according to Dr Christopher Page, Senior Research Fellow in Music at Sidney Sussex College, Cambridge, Hildegard of Bingen can well hold her own. He says that there is no one else like her. She was the first woman composer in Western history. She was truly exceptional, not only among nuns, but among all those who composed religious music in the twelfth century. Her output was large, quite unlike anything else, very individual, and well worth exploring today, both from the musical and from the literary point of view. Hildegard deliberately turned her back on the strict, accentual poetry that was written by men at the time, the *Aeterne rerum conditor* kind of poetry, and decided that her verse should be based much more upon the rhapsodic Latin of the Psalms, or the Song of Songs. Her poetry is close to the Bible, close to liturgy, close to prayer. There is no way of knowing that her songs were ever actually performed in anything like a modern sense. Indeed they may never have been sung at all. It may have been part of Hildegard's exploration of her own spirit, just to write them down.

Hildegard's music shared common cause with her speculations about the material world and the moral philosophy which held it together. She was able, in a way few people are, to pursue her studies in detail and on a grand scale. Tree mallow is good for migraine and the universe is most probably egg-shaped. Nature was not the old enemy awaiting conquest by man. Its strength and its greenness were a sign of the strength of God's love. For Hildegard, philosophy, physics and theology were all one discipline. Pursuit of any branch of knowledge in the created world were inevitably paths to the Creator. This singleness of purpose enabled her to preach to priests, to lecture scholars, to advise popes and to chastise emperors with an authority which no other woman and few men in her age would dare to claim.

Hildegard achieved much, but then, as Dame Felicitas Corrigan says, she began young. When she was four she saw a fireball enter her soul. We think this is far-fetched, but when St Benedict had his famous vision, he was standing in the tower and he saw the soul of the bishop of Capua rising to heaven in a fireball. This is the figure often used to depict the Holy Spirit. Think of the Feast of Pentecost when the Holy Spirit came down in the form of parted tongues of fire, or in the form of fireballs as Hildegard would perhaps say. She had visions which were not visions in our accepted sense. She could use her eyes and do her ordinary work and all the time, in what Meister Eckhart calls the eye of the heart, she was beholding things given to her by the Holy Spirit.

Many prosaic explanations have been given for Hildegard's visions. Perhaps she had acute migraine or scintillating scotoma. That would explain the flashing lights, but not the more complex visions of the New Jerusalem and the communion of saints or the simpler more practical instances of second sight, like being able to divine the colour of an unborn calf. Whatever the source of the visions, there can be no doubt that she used them to get things done in a world hostile to new ideas from women. It would be foolish to portray Hildegard as a knee-jerk radical. In many ways she was highly traditional. She was professed as a Benedictine at the age of eighteen. When her mentor Jutta died, she took over as abbess. Later when she founded her own monastery she insisted on full observance of the Benedictine rule. And, as Brenda Bolton, Senior Lecturer in History at Westfield College, University of London, explains, she did not suffer the less certain gladly. Another abbess near Strasbourg called Hazeka wrote to Hildegard, saying that she was unable to cope with the unruliness of her convent. The nuns were rioting and she wanted to return to a hermit's life. Hildegard was very firm. She said that Hazeka was too unsteady to be a hermit and that her end would be worse than her beginning if she did not rise to the challenge. She told her that she must stay in the convent and grit her teeth.

That may seem hard but Hildegard was living at a time of muscular Christianity. This was the age of the rigorous Bernard of Clairvaux, hailed as the last of the Fathers of the Church. It was also the age of the Knights Templar, the secretive fighting monks dedicated to a life of poverty, chastity, obedience, and killing infidels in the Holy Land. The Knights Templar were founded by Hugh de Payens, a knight from Urban's home territory of Champagne. Initially the idea was that they would police the pilgrim route of Syria and Palestine, but soon the Knights became a military force to be reckoned with, because of an additional vow they took binding them never to flee from the field of battle. Hugh de Payens took his idea to Rome where it was approved.

It was, says Professor Clifford Lawrence, Emeritus Professor of Medieval History at Royal Holloway and Bedford New College, University of London, quickly to acquire a powerful advocate. The Knights asked Bernard to draw up a Rule for them, which he did – a Rule of life for the Templars. He also wrote an apologia for them, because a lot of

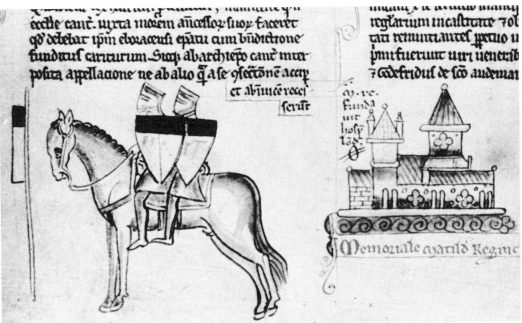

Two Knights Templar (above), *members of the secretive order of fighting monks who took a vow never to flee the field of battle. They would be savagely crushed by Philip the Fair in 1314. St Bernard of Clairvaux* (right), *friend of Hildegard and enemy of Abelard, healing two blind sisters*

people thought that the whole idea of fighting monks was a contradiction in terms. His tract was called *In Praise of the New Knighthood*. It is a highly rhetorical and very emotional piece, appealing to people who were not naturally disposed to become monks to join the Templars.

Bernard, the friend of the Templars, was an intense man. He fired the Second Crusade in the way that Urban fired the First. He was a hymn writer and theologian, passionate in his beliefs and loud in his condemnation of anything he disapproved of, from the persecution of Jews to the corruption of the pope's bureaucracy. He was also generous in his praise of those he approved of, and that, says Brenda Bolton, included Hildegard. Hildegard wrote to Bernard and asked his advice about her visions. He wrote back to her one of the shortest letters he ever wrote – it is only twelve lines. Bernard, we know, did not like even to sit on the same chair that a woman had sat on and was usually very wary of any sort of feminine contact, but he replied and said that he approved her revelations and adjured her to be humble. She must remain humble, but as she had been taught by the Holy Spirit Bernard therefore had nothing to teach her. That must have been quite a boost for her.

From the 1140s Hildegard and her visions were widely known. By 1147 her fame reached the pope's ears and he asked to read her book of visions, the *Scivias*, literally Know the Ways. Those visions were illustrated under her directions by a series of strange symbolic illuminations, a dimension, Dame Felicitas says, which must not be left out from any evaluation of Hildegard. In one of her illuminations, she sees Christ extended on the cross, holding the world in tension – the good and the evil, the light and the darkness. She shows the Cosmic Christ, the Christ not only for Christians. She wrote a wonderful sentence which says that the entire world had been embraced by the Creator's kiss. She uses erotic symbolism and erotic language a good deal. She sees the Cosmic Christ embracing the whole of his creation, kissing and loving it as a husband loves a wife. She sees woman as the feminine element in Christ. Christ suffered in giving us eternal life. Women suffer in giving children life. The experience of Christ and the experience of women cannot be separated, so she sees the enclosed nun stretched out against Christ on the cross, arms to arms, body to body, sustaining all these tensions in the world. She had entered that monastery at eight and had become an enclosed professed nun at eighteen, so Jutta must have been a remarkable abbess to have given her such a through sex education.

Hildegard was not the only one having visions. In Calabria in south Italy, Joachim of Fiore, a Cistercian abbot who is described by a contemporary as having a face like a dried-up leaf, was describing prophetic visions of the whole sweep of history. Like Hildegard, Joachim saw faith as the truth underpinning and making sense of all disciplines. Dr Margory Reeves, formerly Vice-Principal of St Anne's College, Oxford, says that Joachim believed that God was at work throughout the whole of history and that it was in the form of the Trinity that he was manifest. Therefore there were three great stages in the world's history – the stage of the Father, the stage of the Son, and the stage of the Holy Spirit. The exciting aspect of his idea of history was his conviction that the age of the Spirit had not yet fully dawned. It was in the future and this was going to be a great period of illumination. He described these stages in very lyrical terms. He was very poetic and there is one famous passage in his writings in which he says that the age of the Father was the age of the law, the age of the Son was the age of grace, and the age of the Holy Spirit will be the age of liberty, illumination and love. The age of the Father was the age of nettles, the Son roses, and the Holy Spirit lilies. Then he says the Father was water, the Son wine, and the Holy Spirit oil.

At the time Joachim was supported by three popes. Afterwards, some of his teachings would be questioned and rejected. Then as now those claiming prophetic vision would always run the gauntlet of critics. It was of prime importance not to be perceived as claiming personal strength and power. And this, Dr Page believes, holds the key to Hildegard's atrocious health record. Because she was a mystic and a woman she tended to make great play of her own disabilities. It is a tradition in Christian mysticism that if one is somehow impaired in one's physical faculties, this can be seen to be at least the beginning of a testimony towards some special spiritual power. Hildegard is constantly emphasising her headaches, physical aches and pains which have led some modern, especially American, doctors to try and interpret in very specific terms what was actually wrong with her. But she was just following the tradition that if you were physically weak, you were likely to be spiritually strong.

Hildegard composed about seventy-seven hymns and she was also the inventor of the liturgical strike. Dame Felicitas says that she ran into trouble because of her woman's sense of justice. The canons put her under an interdict because she had buried a young revolutionary in her churchyard of St Rupertsberg, and they said that he should not have been buried in consecrated ground. His body had to be taken out and flung onto a heap. She refused. She went down to the cemetery and she covered all the graves so that they all looked alike. You would not have been able to find that young man's grave no matter how you tried. And she said, you have put us under an interdict, you have stopped God's praises completely, so as a result we will mumble – not sing – the office.

Hildegard was not afraid of conflict and there was enough upheaval in the scholarly world of the twelfth century to keep the pugnacious happy. In particular there was a long-nurtured quarrel between Hildegard's correspondent, Bernard of Clairvaux, and a brilliant young cleric teacher from Brittany called Peter Abelard. Professor Clifford Lawrence thinks we have to see this conflict in terms of the rise of the scholastic movement. Abelard was one of the first schoolmen. The intellectual horizons of the twelfth century were raised enormously by the influx of Greek and Arabic science and philosophy becoming available in Latin translation, and by the rise of the secular schools, that is schools with secular clergy rather than monks. All schools were ecclesiastical bodies in the sense that students were clerks, that is members of the clergy, but not necessarily priests in the eyes of canon law. Abelard was a clerk and taught in secular schools but his approach to teaching was that of the new learning. He was one of the first to apply the new logical methods to the data of revealed religion. He was not unorthodox in any sense of the word, but what frightened Bernard was that he would take a dogmatic statement and he would turn it upside-down and shake it up and ask what does this really mean. This frightened Bernard because his approach was very different, he represented the monastic school of theology.

Bernard maintained that logic and faith did not belong together – a view shared by many according to Professor David Luscombe, Professor of Medieval History at Sheffield University, who says that Bernard was not alone. There was a strong current of criticism of Abelard as a teacher both within Paris and outside it. Bernard was persuaded by another Cistercian monk, a man called William of St Thierry, that the problems raised by Abelard in the schools of Paris in the 1130s were a danger to the well-being of the Church at the time, and that the careers and the intellectual health of the students of Paris were being threatened by the teachings of Abelard and his like-minded colleagues. So Bernard intervened. He visited the schools of Paris, where logic and dialectic were being enthusiastically studied and taught, to persuade the students to leave the schools and become monks like himself. He also wrote public treatises and letters in which he explained vigorously what was erroneous about the theological conclusions that Abelard had drawn. He also wrote polemically and powerfully about the need to respect the fact that Christian faith was a matter of experience. It was a matter of living well, it was not meant to be an excuse for disputation and argument. It was not suitable matter for logic chopping.

Bernard conducted a very powerful and certainly very brilliant public letter-writing campaign. He bombarded the pope and the cardinals with letters and also the bishops of France who were responsible for assessing the error or otherwise of Abelard's teaching. The result was an ecclesiastical condemnation for heresy at a Council held at Sens in France in

1140. Although Abelard appealed against the verdict of his episcopal judges, that verdict was upheld by pope Innocent II who ordered that Abelard's books should be burned and that Abelard himself should be confined in a religious place. Abelard, by now a sick man, went into a monastery in Burgundy, the famous monastery of Cluny, where he was befriended by Peter the Venerable. And Peter the Venerable eventually helped to bring Abelard and Bernard to a reconciliation before Abelard died a few years after this terrible setback for him as an intellectual.

But it is what happened between the censure and the reconciliation which is better known. Abelard, the brilliantly aggressive logician, is remembered not for his dialectic, but for his passion and for the vengeance which was wreaked on him. As an additional source of income, Abelard had accepted work tutoring the young niece of Fulbert, a canon of the cathedral in Paris. The girl's name was Eloise. Abelard and Eloise were destined to be the most celebrated lovers of their century and their affair would be one of the most tragic. After Eloise had given birth to a son, Astrolabe, Abelard, who was only in minor orders, married her. Then Abelard made a fateful decision. He was afraid that her uncle would make trouble, so he sent Eloise to the convent where she had been at school. This move was disastrously misinterpreted by Fulbert. He assumed Abelard was adding insult to injury by abandoning Eloise in a convent so that marriage would not get in the way of his academic career. Fulbert decided to repay Abelard in kind. He had him castrated. Eloise never stopped loving him.

Their letters, doubted by some but accepted by many, survive. From them, says Professor Clifford Lawrence, Eloise emerges as much greater than Abelard – a woman of great intellectual power, of enormous human sympathy. Once she had given herself to somebody that was it for life. Abelard's letters are much more formal. He reveals much more of himself in his autobiography, the *Historia Calamitatum*, where he emerges as a highly conceited, arrogant man. Everybody who comes across his path is either a knave or a fool. But even there Eloise pokes through the surface of the autobiography, again as a much greater person. When she became pregnant he decided that he ought to marry her, and she tried to dissuade him. Abelard describes this conversation and it shows that Eloise had a great deal to teach Abelard about the facts of life. She asks, how will you put up with a married household with all the bleating babies and wet nurses. It is all right in the houses of the rich, where you can have a quiet study, but philosophers are not rich. She brings him down to earth. She was a great woman.

After Fulbert's savage revenge, Abelard found shelter at Cluny and friendship from its abbot, Peter the Venerable. When Abelard died, Peter wrote to Eloise describing how Abelard, once acclaimed as the leading

Abelard, the brilliant logician who set the lecture halls of Paris alight with his controversial teaching, with Eloise. Destined to become the most celebrated lovers of their century, their love survived tragedy and separation

scholar of Europe, was so humble in his last days that he only felt happy when he was last in the procession. By this time Eloise was prioress of a convent in Paris. The story of Abelard and Eloise would undoubtedly have been familiar to Hildegard. She had visited the school in Paris with her books under her arm.

And according to Dame Felicitas Corrigan, there is another link between Hildegard the Benedictine and Abelard and Eloise. Eloise and Hildegard were absolute contemporaries. Eloise was the married woman, Hildegard was the virgin. In a famous letter to Abelard, Eloise complains bitterly that there has never been a rule written for nuns, and many of the prescriptions of St Benedict simply do not apply to nuns. How can nuns wear wool next to their skins? Hygiene is against it. Dame Felicitas believes that what Eloise wanted was a rule from her husband. She wanted her husband to rule her monastery as he had once ruled her in Paris.

Hildegard was a great supporter of St Benedict's *Rule*. She always advised adherence to the spirit of the *Rule* rather than slavish observance of the detail. It is a strangely modern approach, but there are many aspects of Hildegard's thought which seem to look beyond her century, for instance her work as a dramatist. Dr Christopher Page says that she wrote one complete play in which all the characters are women. They are virtues which are grammatically feminine. The only man in the play is the devil, *diabolos*, who does not sing, he just shouts – a gift for feminists. Hildegard was steeped in the eight hundred years of Benedictine tradition but like Joachim of Fiore her faith was as much to do with the future as with the past. Brenda Bolton says she was very much part of the twelfth-century renaissance idea, seeing creation as a preparation for the incarnation of Christ, which receives its final perfect fulfilment in the second coming.

She was very much concerned with the future and her forward-looking idea of a profusion of plants and animals and human life under the sway of celestial constellations combined with sacred history is very much part of the twelfth-century renaissance. If you look at the mosaic pavement on the floor of the cathedral at Otranto on the heel of Italy you can see precisely in stone what Hildegard, and indeed many others, were trying to express about their part in the world, the relation of man to God, to his natural world, to things around him. What is extraordinary is how this vast store of astronomical, geological, biological, medical and mystical information that Hildegard brings together in her writings got to a small convent on the Rhine.

However much a backwater Hildegard's convents were, they enabled her to reach conclusions which Dame Felicitas Corrigan believes many of us are only slowly coming to today. Hildegard says the earth is mother of all that is natural, mother of all that is human. Men and women are sprung from the earth which gave substance to the incarnation of the Son of God. She sees this all against a background of revelation which she had learned in her monastery and nowhere else. She talks of the sweating power of the earth, of the need to stay juicy green. Green is one of her favourite words. Be moist, be joyful, she says. She tells people to become a flowering orchard. And she proclaims the beauty of sexuality and marriage. She says that the ultimate sin that man is committing is a sin against God's creation. If we injure the earth, we shall destroy all life including our own. If we ill-treat and violate the elements of the cosmos, misuse the privilege that is ours, then, she says, God's justice will permit creation to punish humanity. Dame Felicitas believes this is what we are seeing now, with the rivers polluted and the air polluted and acid rain and the nuclear threat. Hildegard is remarkable as being the prophet of the twentieth century, the prophet of the ecological age. She saw all creation, the whole cosmos, and this is something we have to recover. She saw that we had to return to a spiritual outlook of gratitude to God for this wonderful cosmos in which we live and she foresaw an age of renewal of the earth as a bio-spiritual planet. She said, if we do not repent, then God's justice, nature itself, will permit creation to punish humanity. She has the sense of earth as a region of delight – a dream for today's world as well as Hildegard's.

THE RICHNESS OF POVERTY

Some thirty years after Hildegard, the great abbess of Bingen, had preached for the last time her visionary message of the sacredness of all the natural world, some thirty years, too, after Eloise had shed her last tear for her life-long love Abelard, Innocent III, a practical pope not given to flights of fancy, had an alarming dream.

> *While the pope slept he saw what he would later describe as a divinely inspired vision. It seemed to him that he was brought before the Basilica of St John Lateran. To his horror he realised that the whole edifice was crumbling. The basilica, which he knew he should understand as a symbol of his whole Church, appeared to be about to collapse while he watched, unable to do anything. Then suddenly, help came from a most improbable source. An insignificant beggarman appeared and put his shoulder to the tottering walls. Incredibly, the feeble poor man was so strong that with his help the mighty basilica did not fall.*

Some days later Innocent was able to make sense of that dream. When Francesco Bernardone, the poor little madman from Assisi, walked into the papal court to seek approval for a new and very old Christian way of life, Innocent recognised in him the beggarman who had saved the church.

Francesco Bernardone, known down the centuries as St Francis of Assisi, was unprepossessing in appearance. He was short, with a smallish head and rather spindly legs. He had thin lips, prominent ears and an unkempt beard but a face which was full of joy. Francis was a mass of contradictions. He came from a rich family, but he chose to be poor. His ideas were revolutionary, all the more so because they were accompanied by a delight in obedience to those in authority. He was a failure in everything but loving God, and that was his great success.

The thirteenth century is above all the century of Francis and his followers. By the end of it there were no fewer than 25,000 Franciscan brothers. It was a time of change and contrast. There was a flowering of learning and commerce, and a shift to urban life. It was also a time of heresy and vision. In the East the Bogomils, who believed Satan was the master of the world, acquired a position of influence in Constantinople. In the West, similar ideas were put forward by the Cathars who taught

that the world was evil. Their leaders were often outstandingly pious men and women, who abstained from meat, eggs, milk and marriage, and who hastened their own deaths by ritual starvation.

The thirteenth century saw crusades in the East *and* the West. Ecclesiastical politics were particularly troubled. The Holy Roman emperor, Frederick II, was accused of dissecting men alive to find out when the soul leaves the body. He was deposed and denounced by the pope, Innocent IV. Later a disastrous and dishonest attempt to heal the Great Schism would reinforce bitterness between the Churches of the East and West. There were Christian wars, and a philosophy for war from the unlikely genius of the slow learner of Aquino, Thomas Aquinas, remembered now as the greatest mind of the medieval church.

This was the world of Francis of Assisi, a world of brutality and idealism, of hardship and romance. And that romance touched every part of Francis's life. He is remembered through numerous contemporary legends – the fearless missionary who walked on coals before the sultan, the gentle holy man who made friends with a ravening wolf, and the fool for God who would not let the flames burning him be put out for fear of harming Brother Fire.

But what of the real Francis, the man who loved marzipan and music played on the fiddle? General Sir Hugh Beach, Assistant Minister Provincial of the Third Order of St Francis, recalls that it was said of him that he was the one true follower of Jesus Christ who has ever lived since that day. He was described by Thomas Celano as a saint among saints, but among sinners he was one of them too. He was totally unselfconscious with anyone he met. His goodness was as of nature, as though there was no dross to overcome. He was full of song and humour and laughter and was anti-money. He embraced what he called his Lady Poverty, and he was violently against any of his followers even touching a coin. They had to beg for their food and live the simplest of all possible lives.

Francis belonged to the newly wealthy merchant class. Ironically the saint who so loathed money had been named after it. His mother had wanted him to be called Pietro after his father, but Pietro Bernardone had other ideas. He decided his son should have a name which celebrated France, the country whose cloth fairs had made the family rich. Francis had a privileged upbringing. As king of feasts in Assisi he was the leader of the social round, but his life of privileged frivolity was soon brought to a halt by the civil warfare which enveloped Assisi. Francis became a cavalry officer, and at the battle of Collestrada he was taken prisoner.

Some months later he was released and took up his old way of life, but disillusionment had set in. He decided to go on crusade but suddenly his ambition to be a knight disappeared.

Brother Terry Tastard of the Society of St Francis says that in his own testament Francis tells us that a major turning point in his life was an incident, probably round about 1205, when he encountered a leper. He had been a young-man-about-town in life, rather proud of his appearance, and for that reason he had been very frightened of lepers and leprosy. One day, in the woods, he came across a leper, and, conquering his initial revulsion and desire to flee, he embraced the man. From then onwards he became somebody who had a special concern for the poor, for those who were needy, for those who were on the margins of society, to such an extent that he himself went to live with the lepers.

Francis returned to Assisi, and at the delapidated chapel of San Damiano he heard a voice coming from the crucifix above the altar. It said 'Francis, repair my house which is falling into ruin'. Francis followed the instructions literally. He began rebuilding the church with his own bare hands. His father was sure his son had become mad. He sued Francis for a bolt of cloth he had taken to cover the expense of rebuilding San Damiano. Finally he publicly disowned his son.

Then Francis was free. He dedicated himself to a life of prayer and poverty. And he inspired others, including a determined young girl from Assisi called Clara Offreducci, who ran away from home to join Francis in his attempt to follow the Gospel literally. But was Clara attracted by the message or by the man?

Sister Agatha, a Franciscan from Brentwood in Essex, thinks both. She believes God uses everything. He takes us on step by step, and we have to have a beginning in our conversion. So He puts the obvious to us, and possibly in Clara's life He put Francis there. He knew from all eternity that Clara was going to serve Him and turn to Him, but she needed something and Francis very quickly steered any emotional growth that might come between them off in another direction. He turned Clara towards Christ. It may have been infatuation to start with when she saw a young man with ideals and bare feet, but it developed into an adventure in faith.

Even in his new life Francis was still influenced by contemporary knightly ideals. He pledged himself to the service of Lady Poverty. In an age of ambition and expansion, Francis was a bewildering reactionary. Brother Terry Tastard doubts that Francis felt at all at home in his society. It was a time of deep and growing divisions between rich and poor. It was a time when quite a large section of the population lived lives of desperate poverty. Francis lived in the middle of a period in which there

Francis preaching to the birds — not an act of eccentricity or sentimentality, but a demonstration of his conviction in the divinity of all the created world

had been an enormous population explosion. Between 1015 and 1300 the population of Europe trebled, so historians tell us, and therefore he lived at a time when there was enormous pressure and he was acutely aware of the desperate plight of people who lived in poverty. From that point of view, he felt very ill at ease whenever he came across ostentatious power or wealth, and he admonished his brothers to avoid anything that would put them in a position of power, even in small details. They must not ride on horseback, for instance.

Francis's uncompromising way of life drew others. He knew some sort of organisation was essential, so with the most rudimentary of rules he set off to gain papal approval for his way of life. In 1206, he went to Innocent with his little scrap of paper. The first words of his rule were to follow the Gospel of our Lord Jesus Christ. And that, says Sister Agatha, is all there is really to the Franciscan rule. It is the Gospel of Christ. When he went to Innocent, the pope had his doubts about the feasibility of such an uncompromising rule, so he prevaricated and said, 'Perhaps you had better come back tomorrow.' Innocent was wise in that he had given himself time and a Benedictine whispered to him and said, 'Look, if you turn away this man, you are really telling the world they cannot live the Gospel because that is all he is asking from you.'

That message hit home and Innocent remembered his dream. The First Order of Franciscans, the minor brothers, received papal approval. Clara and her followers would later form the Second Order. Alone among religious houses for women she secured what was called 'the privilege of poverty' – the right to live solely on gifts without possessing any property. But Francis knew that not everyone could pledge themselves to a life of total poverty. Very early on, his ideals were taken up by lay people; they came to be known as the tertiaries or Third Order of St Francis and they ran into problems as well.

The Reverend Canon David Ford, Canon of Ripon Cathedral, says that in the first few years they were persecuted. They founded leper houses and hospitals, they instituted new standards of honesty in business, and this inevitably brought them into conflict with the business people of the time. They encouraged personal devotion, and we know that the pope had to support them in their endeavours because they were challenging the society of the day. The businessmen did not want honesty in business. They did not want leper colonies. They wanted to forget or to ignore the poor and the suffering and they wanted to get on with business. And therefore it was quite dangerous to be a member of what we would call now the Third Order.

Francis was not the only one preaching poverty. During his early childhood, Peter Waldo of Lyons, formerly a wealthy merchant, was leading his followers on a path of rigorous fidelity to the Gospel and of uncompromising poverty. The Poor Men of Lyons fell foul of Rome and were condemned as heretics. Francis fared better because Innocent III could see the value of the poor men of Assisi. They would be a walking lesson in the living Gospel.

Innocent knew he would never possess the holy madness of Francis but he was in his own way a great man. Michael Walsh, Librarian of Heythrop College, London, says that he was a comparatively holy man as well as a lawyer. Church lawyers are out of fashion nowadays. Everything is now the spirit and love, but the medieval world picture was one that was governed by law and that preserved your rights as well as giving you your duties. In that system Innocent worked very well indeed.

Innocent achieved much but he had his failures too. One of them was the inglorious Fourth Crusade in which Christian knights ransacked Constantinople. Before his death Innocent preached a Fifth Crusade. This gave Francis an opportunity to realise the ambition of his youth. He decided to join the crusaders outside Damietta in Egypt. Brother Terry Tastard says that, like everybody in his day, Francis was convinced that the crusades were something noble and good. But to his credit, as soon as he arrived in Egypt in 1219 he was horrified when he saw their real nature, to such an extent that he went through the ranks of the crusaders at Damietta and told them not to take part in a forthcoming battle. What they were doing, he said, could not be in conformity with the will of God. He was laughed at and scorned for that, but this was typical of the nonconformity of the man and also of his ability to see through the social conventions of the time.

On the same occasion, he risked his life to cross over from the crusader lines to visit the Saracen lines. He spoke only one word of Arabic – 'Sultan, Sultan' – and he crossed over to their side, and crying out 'Sultan Sultan' was brought with a companion into the presence of the sultan himself. The sultan must have been amused at this man dressed in rags who was brought before him and with whom he engaged in a battle of wits. But Francis was living out what he believed most deeply, namely that if you are totally without possessions, totally without power and abandon yourself in trust to God, then you will find that you can go into the most dangerous situations and come out unharmed and in some ways richer for your experiences.

While Francis was in Egypt he heard that at home the Fransiscans were in disarray. During his absence, some friars had tried to water down the demands of literal poverty. Exhausted from his travels and plagued by eye disease contracted in Egypt, Francis turned to the pope as an arbitrator. He was advised that there should be room for both types of Franciscanism. Francis, who only knew that he was called to be a poor madman for God, resigned as leader of the Order.

General Sir Hugh Beach says that in a strange sense Francis was not a natural leader. He was quite happy to hand over the formal leadership of the Order quite early on, to his ex-commanding officer, the man who had been in charge of the Assisian forces at the battle of Collestrada and who was known in the Order as Brother Elias. Brother Elias was a very authoritarian character, at first sight very anti-Franciscan. He believed in great buildings and he erected the most enormous structure at Assisi a couple of years after Francis's death. Why then did Francis let him take over? The answer, says General Beach, is perfectly clear. He was deferring to Elias as his previous commanding officer whom he greatly admired.

The disputes would continue. Whatever modifications were made to the *Rule* it remained a call to poverty. Other options were open. At about the same time Dominic Guzman, a bright-eyed red-haired Castilian, had founded an order of friars whose first purpose was preaching. Why did Dominic not run into the same problems as Francis? Father Simon Tugwell OP, Regent of Studies at Blackfriars, Oxford, says that Francis had a very clear view of what his life was about and he was very clear that nothing was negotiable. So when he found himself really rather at odds with his Order, he could not yield anything because this was all straight from God. Whereas we know that there were certain things that Dominic himself felt very strongly about, things that he wanted to get into the Dominican constitutions, which the brethren did not accept, and there is no hint that there were any troubles over that. Dominic was quite clear that the authority was vested in the brethren and he seems to have trusted them.

He was not glamorous in the way that St Francis is. He was not a man making a point the whole time. He was a very uninhibited person. He used to wake people up at night praying noisily and perhaps because of that they wrote into the constitutions that novices must be taught not to pray noisily. They had had enough of it with Dominic.

For Francis, the handing over of the running of his Order proved to be a great step forward. General Sir Hugh Beach says that from that moment onwards the mystical side of him developed more and more. He was one of those of whom it is said that his attachment and closeness to Christ were such that at one moment of high mystical communion the marks of the cross appeared on his hands and feet and in his side, and he thereafter bore the stigmata. He had a tremendously strong sense of identification with Christ and this governed all the later years of his life. But even that went with a sense of humour. He has been described as the first poet in the Italian language, and right towards the end of his life when he was desperately ill, in great pain and blind, he wrote a beautiful canticle, *The Sun*, a marvellous outpouring of love and joy and unity with creation. In the latter years of his life when all the military side had fallen away, when he was disillusioned with the Order that he had created because it was going away from his own ideals, he became not only a saint among saints but also a mystic among mystics.

One of the crusades which Francis had no hand in was the crushing of the Cathar or Albigensian heretics in France. Dominic and his followers had been involved in the preaching mission to the Albigensians which preceded the crusade. They also became identified with one of the most sinister legacies of the Middle Ages – the Inquisition, the church courts designed to root out heresy. But why was the Church so afraid of the

St Dominic, the founder of the Order of Preachers and noisy nocturnal prayer presiding over the burning of heretical books

Albigensians? Father Simon Tugwell says that the Albigensian heresy, as a matter of doctrine, was a form of dualism. It taught there was a good god who made the things we approve of, somebody else made the things we do not like, but how far that doctrine was successful in percolating through to the Albigensian hangers-on is anybody's guess. There seems to have been a lot of superstition and a lot of simple admiration for good people. Its leaders were undoubtedly remarkable men and women. The real point of controversy centred on Catholicism because it was very easy to argue that the Catholic Church, and particularly the clergy, were manifestly not the Church of Jesus Christ. The arguments seem to have been more a matter of persuading people that there was a good case that could be made in favour of the Catholic Church, rather than in showing up the absurdity of heretical doctrine. Recent work on the Inquisition has tended to suggest that, far from giving people hell where they were not getting hell before, the Inquisition was actually instituting proper juridical procedure so that people were not being given hell by the mob. People were being lynched before. The Inquisition stopped people being lynched. There was now a proper procedure for heretic hunting.

The Albigensian Crusade and the Inquisition would leave bitter memories. Later in the century, with Charles of Anjou threatening a crusade against Constantinople, the Churches of the East and West would receive another setback. This was the disastrously bungled attempt at healing the Great Schism through a Council at Lyons. Professor Donald Nicol, Emeritus Professor of Modern Greek and Byzantine History at King's College, London, explains that was a put-up job. The delegation that went from Constantinople in 1274 was very small and very unrepresentative of Byzantine opinions or indeed of Byzantine theology or politics. They took a document with them from the emperor, Michael VIII Palaeologus, and presented it to the pope, Gregory X. It said all the things that the pope wanted to hear – that the Schism was now mended, and that the Byzantines, or Greeks, fully agreed with the Roman form of the Creed including the addition to the Creed and therefore the split between the Churches was over. There was no discussion, no debate, just the signing of documents which was what the pope wanted, and the pope then said to Charles of Anjou: 'Right, your crusade is off. I cannot authorise a crusade against fellow Christians,' which is what the Eastern emperor wanted him to say. Charles of Anjou was so cross he bit the top off his sceptre.

There was no debate. The patriarch of Constantinople, John Beckos, thought his way round to approving of the union with Rome and said so. He and the emperor were afterwards condemned by the whole Orthodox Church as heretics. When Michael VIII died in December 1281, the Church would not give him a proper burial. His corpse was left on a mountainside for some time and later legend had it that it blew up like a drum, which is a sure mark of having died in heresy. It refused to rot – even the earth rejected it.

For all the gentleness of Francis, the thirteenth-century Church was inured to violence. War was a tool of ecclesiastical politics. And a Dominican friar, Thomas of Aquino, Thomas Aquinas, set out to do the impossible – to define the causes of a just war. General Sir Hugh Beach explains that what he said was quite categoric. It is not lawful to kill an innocent person, one who is doing no harm, children, old people, people playing no part in the war. The guilty, those who are war-makers, can only be killed when they can clearly be separated from the innocent. If you are going to bomb a city, to destroy a factory, and you are going to destroy a lot of innocent civilians thereby, then, according to Thomas, that is wrong. That is a very stiff test indeed and has been most conspicuously transgressed. It is crucially important, in view of all the arguments today about the permissibility or otherwise of a nuclear war. The criterion that most people latch onto is that which is called proportionality. What he said was that, if the harm you do in the war is greater than that good you are securing by waging that war, then you must not do it. You must sue for peace, you must stop, you must not go to war in the first instance. This is centre stage when it comes to talking about the nuclear weapon because its proponents say that the good that is intended by the possession of nuclear weapons is the prevention of nuclear war, the prevention of all war, and this is a good which is admirably proportioned to the evils of possession which so far have been very low. But the counter argument to that is that if it came to war the evils created would be almost immeasurable and could not possibly be proportioned to any good. So there is this great intellectual dilemma and on that Thomas only gets us part of the way, but at least he has set out the vital arguments with matchless clarity.

Thomas Aquinas was in precise contrast to St Francis. He stands as a man of enormous erudition, of enormous learning, of enormous intellectual influence, affecting the intellectual life of the church to this day.

Often both Francis and Dominic and their mendicant, that is begging, orders are seen as revolutionaries – a view challenged by Alexander Murray, Fellow and Praelector in Modern History at University College, Oxford, who believes there is quite another way of looking at it. Look at the Orders from the point of view of a bishop and a very different picture emerges. It is all rather similar to the health services today in Great Britain. If you have a problem you take it to the family doctor, but should he not have enough time then the first link of the chain is broken and everything grinds to a halt. So, in the late twelfth century, the theologians of Paris really started getting down to the practical consequences of Christianity and working out a system that would actually function in the budding society of their day. Pope Innocent III put many of his fellow students from the time when he had himself been a student in Paris into the bishoprics and said, let us make this Church work according to the new

St Thomas Aquinas, the Dominican friar who attempted the impossible – the definition of the just war

structure. At this point, they came up against a figure called a parish priest, on whom the whole system rested. Now to say that all the priests were corrupt would be just a sweeping generalisation doing much injury to any of these heroes who sat there doing their work properly. But the parish priest was a celibate character, living alone in a community which in some respects was still very barbaric. How could he have been expected to stand up against all the pressures of the work around him? The mendicant Orders come in at this point. The mendicant convents were rather carefully positioned, as urban archaeology has shown, near the entrances to the towns, or near the city wall. A study of this urban archaeology together with certain papal bulls shows that what the bishops had in mind was to use the mendicant Orders to cure two problems at once. On one hand, they would provide new parishes for the housing estates near the city walls. Secondly, they would provide new super-parishes. It often happens in technology that if, for example, you need a new railway line, you get the up-to-date version. In the same way, the new parishes, which were not really parishes but pastoral services, were provided in the new, up-to-date version. And what was this? A group of dedicated people, who had taken vows of poverty, chastity and obedience, who lived together under a common rule so that they could keep an eye on each other and keep each other company. When they came back after a tiring day, they had their community which supported them. They were all supposed to study theology, so that they knew what they were talking about. If they had to preach they knew what they had to preach. And if, while hearing confession, which was coming in during the thirteenth century on quite a big scale, somebody came up with some sin or other, the Franciscans and the Dominicans would generally know what to say. In a word, the mendicant Orders appear to have been the answer of the Church, as led by its bishops, to a pressing pastoral problem. This was composed on one side of the new urban populations and on the other of the difficulty of keeping going, in practice, a system in which a parish priest was supposed to bear the whole weight of the pastoral church on his own shoulders. If it were not for the Church and the bishops, we never would have heard of the Franciscan Order.

Francis's death was even more simple than his life. In his last years he suffered greatly from gastric ulcers and fevers which were most probably recurrent bouts of malaria. His eye conditions worsened, and it was not improved by the ministrations of the papal physicians who cut and cauterised all veins from his ears to his eyebrows. Once Francis knew he was dying he was happy. He sent a farewell letter to Clara, sang songs, and asked for his favourite marzipan and for a fiddle to be played to him. Just before the end he instructed his friars to strip him naked and lay him on the ground. Some say that as he died a flight of skylarks soared across the sky. His had been a short life, lived out with a dedication and extremism which few would be able to emulate but many would be inspired by up to today.

His fame has spread more than that of any other saint. Canon David Ford says that somehow Francis did not see material *things*, he saw God in everything, in all creation. One of the problems for any Christian is the difficulty of being pulled in several directions: do you do the will of God and what is it? Or do you hang on to certain securities or abilities or possessions? Francis saw even academic ability as a possession and he did not approve of some of the friars becoming academics or teaching in universities because that knowledge could become a possession of theirs and therefore take them away from God. In the Book of Ecclesiastes (Chapter 7, verse 29), the words of the Scriptures say that God has made us plain and simple, but we made ourselves very complicated. Francis is true to that. We really are, deep in our spiritual selves, childlike, children of God, but we complicate things and we spoil things by our own works. Francis asks us not to.

HELL, PURGATORY AND PARADISE

.

In the year 1300, long after the poor little madman of Assisi had preached his last sermon of poverty and simple joy, a middle-aged Florentine politician and poet began a visionary journey of such grandeur and complexity that it puzzled, terrified and inspired his contemporaries and today offers us an unparalleled insight into, and summary of, the religious beliefs of all the Christian Centuries which preceded it. The journey, like many important journeys, began when the traveller was completely lost. Wandering through a dark forest, he was suddenly confronted by a tall archway with a deadly inscription.

Through me is the way to the city of woe
Through me is the way to eternal pain
Through me lies the way to a people forever lost

All hope abandon ye who enter here.

The traveller, an ascetic, almost haunted-looking man, with a fiercely aquiline nose and a forbidding downturned mouth was Dante Alighieri, a poet hailed by some as the father of European literature, a philosopher believed by others to have been to hell and back on an adventure of faith and reason.

Dante was born in 1265 of an ancient and noble Florentine family. He fell in love when he was nine with Beatrice Portinari. His love for Beatrice and his devotion to his city would dominate his life. But those feelings were destined to become more than *personal* emotions. In the early years of the fourteenth century Dante drew on both these loyalties to begin his life's chief work, the *Divina Commedia*, an exploration of hell, purgatory and paradise, and the greatest Christian allegory ever written.

The year 1300 was declared a Holy Year by pope Boniface VIII, a man whom Dante loved to hate. The century was destined to be one of glory, revolt, epidemics and war. Dante, looking back to the great minds of antiquity and forward to all our futures, stands on the hinge of a world of transition. Reform and renaissance are waiting in the wings. Dante, imbued with the old ideals of courtly love, would have to survive a harsh world of political tension and rivalry. Church and State would have to

Dante – an almost haunted-looking man on his visionary journey from hell, through purgatory to paradise

come to terms with incipient nationalism. The century would encompass the savagery of the crushing of the Templars, the wisdom of the quietists of the East and the commonsense gentleness of an Englishwoman from Norwich.

Throughout Dante's lifetime Christians as usual were at loggerheads with Christians. But there was one place at least where they could meet on common ground and that was on the threshold of Dante's menacing archway – the entrance to hell. Throughout the Christian world there was an unswerving belief in the reality of the after-life. Dante was not dealing with the arcane. He was dealing with the commonplace. When Dante's corpse went temporarily missing after his death, many people assumed that it was perfectly natural that in death he must be making the same bodily journey which he had been privileged to make in his lifetime. And in his lifetime it had been remarked that you could see in his face that he had been burnt by the fires of hell. A facile view – or is it? Is the *Divina Commedia* solidly based on physical fact or is it beautiful fiction expressing profound truth but unrelated to any real experience?

Dr Christopher Ryan, part-time Lecturer in the Department of Italian at Cambridge University, believes Dante drew on more than fiction – and more than fact. Dante, he says, undoubtedly had an experience of enormous impact and importance. Just as for most people that spiritual experience would have an imaginative component, it would either take place in a dream or would stimulate the imagination in some sense. Dante in the journey describes things in such immense detail that at times it is difficult to believe that he was not somewhere comparable to the place he is describing. He was an immensely imaginative man, and therefore if he had an enormously important and deep spiritual experience, that would undoubtedly have a very vivid imaginative component. Whatever the core of that imaginative component was, Dante was able to develop it into a description of the three realms of Hell, Purgatory and Paradise with imaginative and artistic integrity.

Dante's journey through the three realms of the after-life begins with a descent into the circles of Hell. His guide is Virgil, the classical poet, who described Aeneas' journey to Hades and whose predictions of a saviour child had earned him the fanciful accolade of being the pagan prophet of Christianity. But it is clear that Dante's inspiration was Beatrice, his childhood love, who had died ten years before he began writing the *Divina Commedia*. Dante describes her as the blest spirit sent from heaven to give him the courage to follow Virgil through Hell. Later she would be his guide through Paradise.

But is it possible to fall in love for life at the age of nine? Dr Brian Horne, Lecturer in Christian Doctrine at King's College, London, thinks that is a moot question. It is certainly possible to have an extraordinarily profound, emotional experience as early as that, especially experiences of love. Beatrice was a year or so younger than Dante was. He only met her three times after the first time. They never married, they never made love. Two of those occasions were painful occasions for Dante when she rebuked him, and she died probably in the year 1290. Two or three years after her death he wrote his first book, the *Vita Nuova*, the new life, in which he talks about his meeting with her, and she becomes the inspiration for his great work, the *Divina Commedia*. His relationship with her was something which was at the very centre of his being. Beatrice is the beginning of his salvation and almost the end of his salvation – almost because his salvation is God. She is the channel through which he comes to be saved, to arrive at the vision of the Trinity at the end of the *Divina Commedia*.

Dante depicts his love for Beatrice as more than the love of one person for another. He reserves the second circle of Hell for the great romantic lovers of the past. Dido, Helen, Cleopatra, Achilles, Paris and Francesca of Rimini spend eternity in darkness buffeted by fierce winds. They are in Hell because they have been content with romantic love and were unable to see further than the object of their affection and desire. Dante believed love should become a celebration of reason. It is the most powerful guarantor of morality and defence against sin. For Dante, love, once inspired, should have the widest and most altruistic implications.

Dr Christopher Ryan says that Dante regarded the impulse of love as being absolutely at the centre of the universe and of the human being, and that single impulse of love articulated itself in different ways in love for the individual and in love for the community. And Dante made the very commonsense observation that love of the community cannot at the end of the day be divorced from political considerations. So it was not that he had a private life and a public life and these were very distinct. On the contrary, Dante would want to say that the single impulse of love was what guided both the individual conduct and public conduct. Nor was this love separate from Christian love. One of the most interesting things about Dante is precisely the way in which he thought the single impulse of love was involved both in Christianity and in the whole of human life. Dante does not get the admiration he should as a religious thinker.

After Dante has travelled through the nine circles of hell, and met gluttons, heretics, tyrants, murderers, frauds and traitors, he climbs the mountain of Purgatory where those who have died loving God are cleansed of their sin. At the top of the mountain he comes to the flower-strewn forest of the Earthly Paradise and there he meets Beatrice who will guide him through the spheres of heaven. Their conversation, Dr Brian Horne believes, contains the key to a forgotten answer to one of the most basic questions of life.

When Beatrice meets Dante at the top of the mountain of Purgatory, in the Earthly Paradise, almost her first words to him are, 'Look, I am really Beatrice,' and then she says, 'How did you dare climb this mountain? Did you not know that men are happy here?' This is astonishing. She does not say saved, or holy, or gracious, or pure, she says happy. If you go back to Thomas Aquinas and read his treatise on the end of man, Thomas says that the end for which human beings were created is happiness, and this is precisely what Dante is saying here. This strain of medieval theology has rather been lost sight of.

Dante and Beatrice – Dante's love for Beatrice lasted all his life and inspired his finest work

But how do you quantify perfect happiness? A question Dante put to the spirit of Piccarda Donati whom he meets in the sphere of moon, the lowest realm of Paradise. Dr Alexander Murray says Dante sees Paradise stretching away nearer and nearer to the Creator as the levels of the celestial hotel get higher and higher nearer to the Creator. And he says to Piccarda, 'Down there you are supposed to be in eternal bliss at this point, but I have a problem. Surely the people nearer to God up there are in greater bliss.' And Piccarda says, 'No you have got it wrong,' and there is a beautiful passage where she explains that the joy of the souls in heaven derives from the vision of celestial harmony which includes celestial justice. And therefore, if you were to be put in heaven above the place which is proper to you according to your deserts and the degree and manner of your life on earth, you will perceive this instantly as a soul in heaven as a blemish on the exercise of divine justice, and your pleasure would thereby be diminished.

Dante insists that Christian love cannot be separated from justice. This is why a loving God can sanction the punishment of sinners and why here on earth Christians should fight injustice. So much for theory. While Dante was writing the *Divina Commedia*, Christian Europe was shaken by a murderous conspiracy executed with papal collusion. Even in a violent age it soon became a byword for inhuman cruelty and all too human greed. It was the stamping out of the Order of Knights Templar, the fighting monks who had protected the pilgrim route and fought the infidel in the East. Many accusations would be levelled against them, from charges of sodomy to allegations of bizarre pagan ritual involving the worship of a severed head. But Professor Clifford Lawrence believes they owed their demise to something far more mundane. They had become too rich.

The Knights had many establishments in Western Europe to raise money which was then channelled out to the fighting troops in the Middle East. As they lost their role in the crusading principalities they became more and more like international bankers of the Mediterranean. They performed the role of a medieval Securicor service. They acted as creditors to travellers and they lent money to kings. People do not generally love their creditors, and in the end it was this that attracted the hate of Philip the Fair of France. When he launched his great attack in the year 1307, he was just after their money. The whole affair was a piece of outrageous skulduggery.

Dante protested loudly against the treatment of the Templars. Ian Wilson, author and historian, thinks he did it because he was convinced the Templars had indeed been innocent. But it was too late because Philip the Fair had been all too efficient and Dante was just a voice crying after the event. First of all, at dawn on Friday 13 October 1307 Philip the Fair had the Templars arrested by his marshals, who were given sealed orders right throughout France. Then the Dominicans were set to work as good inquisitors and every element of torture was used. There are horrendous stories of one Templar holding up two bones from his feet as a result of having been roasted over a fire too much. They confessed to all sorts of different things and a lot of the charges were sexual. And then in the most dramatic circumstances of all, four of the leading Templars were brought out to be sentenced to life imprisonment in 1314.

The deal was that they were supposed to repeat publicly before the papal commissions and the cardinals that they had indeed done all the dirty deeds that they had been charged with. Two of them said that they had and went off to be perpetually imprisoned, but the Grand Master,

Jacques de Mollay, and the Master of Normandy, Geoffrey de Chané, stunned everyone by suddenly getting up and saying that the Order was pure and holy, that they had done nothing wrong, and that they had only said that the Order had heinous malpractices because of the tortures they had been subjected to. Philip the Fair acted with characteristic swiftness. He immediately had the two condemned to be burnt at the stake and they went to their deaths very forcefully, proclaiming the Order's innocence to all around them. They also called upon the Almighty to bring down suitable justice upon Philip the Fair and pope Clement V. It is a matter of historical fact that those two both died rather unpleasant deaths within the year. A few Templars survived in England but the Order was to all intents and purposes dead.

Generally in England in the fourteenth century there was a flowering of spirituality. The anonymous author of *The Cloud of Unknowing* and the Oxford-educated hermit mystic Richard Rolle have both recently enjoyed something of a revival. Most of all the revelations of anchoress Julian of Norwich are now more widely known than ever they were in her lifetime. Some of her teaching sounds implausibly modern. Was she the first feminist theologian?

Dr Grace Jantzen, Lecturer in the Philosophy of Religion at King's College, London, says that when Julian sees God as mother, it is not a kind of fourteenth-century feminism, but a recognition that God is the one who brings us to birth. That is one important aspect of her theology. Another closely related aspect is the way in which the wounding, the brokenness and fragmentation that we experience can be made into honours, as she puts it, into the badges of glory. As the wounds of Jesus become the ways in which we see his glory, so also the wounding of our personality – through mother Jesus, as she says – can be made ways in which we are more sensitive, in which we are more open, more whole people.

In terms of her understanding of God as Trinity, when Julian talks about God as mother, she is referring first of all to Jesus as our mother. Jesus is our creator, so we have our original birth in him, Jesus is the one who dies and thereby redeems us and gives us our second birth in him, and Jesus, like a mother, feeds us with his own body and blood. It is interesting that in the Middle Ages it was thought that a mother's milk was blood that had been processed through her body, so the blood of the Eucharist could be seen as the nourishing that Jesus gives us.

Richard Rolle, Julian's contemporary, based his mystic teaching on meditation on the name of Jesus. His writings were widely known and respected in Western Europe. Eastern mystics fared less well. On Mount Athos a high-born monk called Gregory Palamas became the most famous

*Pope Clement V. Together with pope Nicholas III he was placed in hell by Dante.
Adrian V was luckier – he was put in purgatory*

exponent of a system of meditation called hesychasm, which involved a
quietening of body, mind and spirit. He taught that posture and breathing
were part of prayer. Gregory's teachings were controversial but eventually
accepted by the Church of the East where he was canonised as a Doctor
of the Church. However, his ideas, in our day rediscovered by the West
through non-Christian religions, were boorishly rejected by some Western
Christians.

Professor Donald Nicol says that Gregory Palamas' views on hesychasm had been ridiculed and held up to contempt by people who did not
understand what it was all about. One of them was a half-westernised
monk from the south of Italy called Barlarm who was himself a scholar
and a philosopher and had given some highly successful lectures in
Constantinople. He fell out with Gregory Palamas and he took to ridicu-
ling this method of prayer. Part of the Palamas method was to sit in a
particular posture, literally staring at your navel, and repeating the words
'Jesus Christ have mercy on me, a sinner' over and over again. The Jesus
Prayer as it is called. And Barlarm went to town on this, and made a great
mock of it all, and referred to the hesychasts as men who keep their souls
in their navels.

Dante had no doubt about the value of meditation. He places con-
templatives and ascetics in the seventh sphere of Heaven. But he sounds
a warning note. He meets St Benedict the father of Western monks who
decries the corruption of contemporary monasteries. He also meets Peter
Damian the severe monastic reformer who believed that bishops should
not play chess. Peter Damian voices scathing criticism of the comfortable
lives of some bishops and cardinals – a sign of discontent to come. The
religious map of Europe was about to be redrawn, and Dante's decision
to write the *Divina Commedia* in Italian as opposed to Latin was part of
the tide of change. As Dr Christopher Ryan says, in a sense Dante is
summing up an aspiration of the Middle Ages which is to express beautiful
things beautifully – in this case the beauty of God. And yet he is also
pushing forward, because although there are masterpieces of religious
expression in the Middle Ages written in Latin, Dante is unique in giving
the quality of thought and the quality of linguistic expression in the young
language. He is also pushing forward into the whole vernacular culture
that was growing up and would flower later in the Renaissance and
beyond.

Dante was far from a revolutionary but contemporary figures he
claimed to have met in Hell caused a few eyebrows to be raised. His

theology was not radical but some of his politics were – particularly his understanding of the political role of the pope as expressed in his *De Monarchia*. Dr Brian Horne says that what he was proposing was a complete separation of the temporal and the ecclesiastical powers – a complete separation between the papacy and the government of the world. It was extremely unpopular with medieval popes and Dante was looked upon with some suspicion after his death. He nourished and cultivated implacable hatreds against certain ecclesiastical rulers because he thought that they were perverting the proper business of the Church in assuming political power. And when he came to write the *Divina Commedia*, he placed several ecclesiastics in the Inferno, including his great enemy pope Boniface VIII.

Nicholas III and Clement V were also placed in the eighth circle of Hell by Dante. Adrian V was luckier – he was put on the fifth terrace of Purgatory. Dante was no heretic with a feud against the papacy. His beliefs about the necessary separation of Church and State were part of a much larger movement. Dr Alexander Murray says that to speak of heresy is to use a label which is dangerous and misleading, but Dante would never have written and would not have been read if there had not been, not only in the Italian cities but all over Europe, a lot of people who appreciated Dante's belief that the papacy had degenerated. Indeed he believed the Church as a whole had fallen from the simple ideals of Peter the Fisherman and the simple apostolic examples of the early days into a state of political corruption and greed, heavily infected by the standards of the world.

Dante was no ecclesiastical anarchist. His faith was nothing if not structured and orthodox. As part of the Church, he cared enough to criticise it loudly. His faith was based on the love of God which touches all lives and must be larger than any ecclesiastical bureaucracy. As Dr Christopher Ryan says, Dante was not that kind of layman who is most at home when he is surrounded by clerics and cathedrals. Dante was someone who began as a love poet who lived his life in the rough and tumble of politics and diplomacy thereafter, but who was constantly engaged in thinking and in reading. Dante actually came quite late to philosophic and theological studies, and this shows in his conception of Christianity. For him, working out of the love poetry and the love ethic, he came to see Christianity as being the re-creation of the original impulse to love that had been present from the beginning in creation. So in Dante's mind, Christianity is helping to re-create the original impulse of love given

Julian of Norwich, the English anchoress and mystic who taught about the motherhood of God

JULIAN of
NORWICH

in creation, and therefore it is a false dichotomy to see in Dante anything like a break between his secular love and his religious love, because he saw both of them as the articulation of a single impulse.

In the final cantos of the *Divina Commedia*, Dante progresses through the highest reaches of Paradise. Finally with St Bernard as his guide he is granted a vision of the brightness of the mystery of God. There he sees all leaves scattered throughout the universe bound in a single volume of love. He gazes on the Trinity, three circles and one, and strains to describe that single triune force of love by which divinity expressed itself through humanity and the spirit where all life and one life meet.

> *My powers failed that towering fantasy*
> *But yet my desire and will were rolled onward*
> *Like a wheel of even motion, impelled by love*
> *That love which moves the sun and all other stars*

Those words, the last stanzas of the *Divina Commedia*, were only discovered after Dante's death. From that day to this, Dante's journey has fascinated those who share his religious beliefs and also those who do not. Why? Dr Brian Horne thinks there are various answers to that question. The first was given by Dorothy Sayers, when she says that it is a marvellous narrative – the journey through the terrors and the horrors of Inferno, the escape of Dante and his guide, Virgil, out of Inferno, up the mountain of Purgatory, into the Earthly Paradise, the meeting with Beatrice, the travelling through the circles of Paradise, up to the Vision of the Trinity at the end. So it is at that level a great story and it has attracted many people simply because of the story. Secondly, there is the sheer technical mastery of Dante writing in this Italian at this time, and the richness of the imagery. It is as though all the sights and the sounds of late medieval Europe flowed through this *Divina Commedia*. Time after time he will use an image that actually conjures up a street in Florence, or the birds across the marshes, when he is actually making a theological point, or trying to describe a most difficult scene in Purgatory. So there is this mastery as well. And thirdly, there is his immense grasp of theology. It is the theological structure of the *Divina Commedia* that is of such interest, not only to poets and to artists, but to theologians. What he is doing is simply perfecting the Christian vision – the theology of the fourteenth and fifteenth centuries – by means of his poetic gift. Dante completes the Christian Centuries which had gone before.

Dante like many before him stood on the edge of something more beautiful than his words – something larger than his dreams. In his journey through the after-life he met many who have played their part in the Christian Centuries. He stands at the end of the Middle Ages. He knew a

Church which had been dominant and at times domineering and needed reform. He bound together the pre-Christian past and a Christian vision of each believer's future. He describes a vocation of happiness, love and justice – a dream and vision which then as now is surely worth realising.

CONTRIBUTORS

Sister Agatha, a Franciscan from Brentwood, Essex

Dr Donald Allchin, St Saviour's Centre for Christian Spirituality in Oxford

Mashuq Ally, Lecturer in Religious Studies and Director of the Centre of Islamic Studies at St David's University College, Lampeter

Metropolitan Anthony, Head of the Russian Orthodox Church in Great Britain and Ireland

General Sir Hugh Beach, Assistant Minister Provincial of the Third Order of St Francis

Brenda M. Bolton, Senior Lecturer in History at Westfield College, University of London

Mr Gerald Bonner, Reader in Theology at the University of Durham

Professor Robert Browning, Emeritus Professor of the University of London

Professor A. A. M. Bryer, Director at the Centre for Byzantine, Ottoman and Modern Greek Studies at Birmingham University

Professor D. A. Bullough, Professor of Medieval History at St Andrews University, Scotland

Professor Averil Cameron, Professor of Late Antique and Byzantine Studies and Director of the Centre for Hellenic Studies, King's College, London

The Revd Professor Henry Chadwick, Regius Professor Emeritus of Divinity and Master of Peterhouse, Cambridge

Professor Owen Chadwick, Chancellor of the University of East Anglia and formerly Master of Selwyn College, Cambridge

Russell Chamberlain, author and biographer of Charlemagne

Dame Felicitas Corrigan OSB, Benedictine nun of Stanbrook Abbey in Worcestershire

Revd H. E. J. Cowdrey, Senior Research Fellow in Modern History at St Edmund Hall, Oxford

Revd Douglas Dales, Chaplain and Head of Religious Studies at Marlborough College, Wiltshire

Dr Hilda Davidson, formerly Vice-President of Lucy Cavendish College, Cambridge, and Lecturer in Anglo-Saxon and Norse Studies

The Revd Professor J. Gordon Davies, Professor Emeritus of Theology at University of Birmingham

Dr Gillian Evans, Lecturer in the Faculty of History and Fellow of Fitzwilliam College, Cambridge

The Revd Canon D. G. Ford, Residentiary Canon of Ripon Cathedral

Dr Simon Franklin, Fellow of Clare College, Cambridge

The Revd Professor William Frend, Professor Emeritus of Ecclesiastical History at Glasgow University

Dr Sergei Hackel, Vicar General of the Russian Orthodox Church in Great Britain

The Revd Professor S. G. Hall, Professor of Ecclesiastical History at King's College, London

Dr Judith Herrin, Visiting Professor at Princeton University in the USA

Dr Brian Horne, Lecturer in Christian Doctrine in the Department of Christian Doctrine and History, King's College, London

Cardinal Basil Hume OSB, Roman Catholic Archbishop of Westminster

Dr D. Hunt, Lecturer in the Department of Classics and Ancient History at the University of Durham

Dr Grace Jantzen, Lecturer in the Philosophy of Religion in the Department of History and Philosophy of Religion, King's College, London

Revd Dr J. N. D. Kelly, Honorary Fellow of St Edmund Hall, Oxford

Mr Robin Lane Fox, Fellow and Tutor in Ancient History at New College, Oxford

Professor C. H. Lawrence, Emeritus Professor of Medieval History at Royal Holloway and Bedford New College, University of London

Mr Andrew Louth, Senior Lecturer in Religious Studies at Goldsmiths' College, London

Professor D. E. Luscombe, Professor of Medieval History at University of Sheffield

Dr Rosamond D. McKitterick, Fellow of Newnham College, Cambridge

Professor John MacQueen, University Endowment Fellow at the School of Scottish Studies at the University of Edinburgh

Professor C. Mango, Bywater and Sotheby Professor of Byzantine and Modern Greek Language and Literature at Exeter College, Oxford

Professor R. A. Markus, Emeritus Professor of Medieval History at the University of Nottingham

Dr John Matthews, Fellow and Praelector in Ancient History, Queen's College, Oxford

Sister Charles Murray, Lecturer in Historical Theology in the Department of Theology at the University of Nottingham

Dr Alexander Murray, Fellow and Praelector in Modern History at University College, Oxford

Dr J. L. Nelson, Lecturer in History at King's College, London

Professor Donald M. Nicol, Emeritus Professor of Modern Greek and Byzantine History, King's College, London

Sir Dimitri Obolensky, Fellow in Byzantine and East European History, Christ Church, Oxford

Dr Christopher Page, Senior Research Fellow in Music at Sidney Sussex College, Cambridge

Dr Marjory Reeves, formerly Vice-Principal of St Anne's College, Oxford, and leading authority on Joachim of Fiore

Professor J. Riley-Smith, Head of the Department of History at the Royal Holloway and Bedford New College, University of London

Dr J. M. Roberts, Warden of Merton College, Oxford

Dr Christopher Ryan, part-time Lecturer in the Department of Italian at the University of Cambridge

Professor Ihor Ševčenko, Dumbarton Oaks Professor of Byzantine History and Literature at Harvard University

Revd Michael A. Smith, Church Historian and Baptist Minister of Golcar in West Yorkshire

Revd Dr Kenneth Stevenson, author and liturgist

Brother Terry Tastard, Society of St Francis

Father Simon Tugwell OP, Regent of Studies, Blackfriars, Oxford

Father F. X. Walker SJ, Head of the Department of Ecclesiastical History at Heythrop College, London

Michael Walsh, librarian at Heythrop College, London

Dom Henry Wansbrough OSB, monk at Ampleforth Abbey, Yorkshire

Sister Benedicta Ward SLG, Lecturer in History and Religion at the Centre for Medieval and Renaissance Studies, Oxford

Bishop Kallistos Ware, Bishop of the Greek Orthodox Church

Dr John Wilkinson, Canon of St George's, Jerusalem

Mr Ian Wilson, author and historian

Mr N. G. Wilson, Tutor in Classics and Fellow of Lincoln College, Oxford

Dr Ian N. Woods, Senior Lecturer in the Department of Medieval History at the University of Leeds

Dr C. P. Wormald, Lecturer in the Department of Medieval History at the University of Glasgow

Mr David R. Wright, Senior Lecturer in Ecclesiastical History and Dean of the Faculty of Divinity at the University of Edinburgh

Father Edward Yarnold SJ, Tutor in Theology, Campion Hall, Oxford

INDEX

·

PICTURE CREDITS

.